365 DAYS
OF
KNITTING

365 Knitting Patterns for 365 Days

White Lemon

365 Days of Knitting

Disclaimer

No part of this publication may be reproduced in any form or by any means, including printing, photocopying, or otherwise without prior written permission of the copyright holder. If you would like to use material from the book (other than just simply for reviewing the book), prior permission must be obtained by contacting the author.

Contents

January

February

March

April

May

June

July

August

September

October

November

December

INTRODUCTION

Knitting can be a great way to relax, and you can also get a lot accomplished. A lot of people think that they can't create beautiful knitted items, because it is just too difficult. While there are some pretty intricate and complicated patterns out there, you will also find thousands of patterns that are super-easy to re-create. Many patterns can actually be made up in a few hours. For instance, you can make dishcloths, scarves, and a lot more, using basic knit and purl stitches. After a while, you will find that you want to take it to the next level and learn how to do some of the fancier stitches and patterns.

This e-book is ideal for the beginning knitter, and for those who are looking for quick and easy projects. You will find an easy pattern for every day of the year. Of course, there will be some extra-special holiday patterns, as well as patterns for everyday items, bridal items, clothing, and a whole lot more. Don't feel like you have to do each and every pattern, or that you have to do them in any particular order (except for a few that are two items made to go together). We want you to have fun and learn the joy of knitting, at your own pace.

In addition to patterns, you will also find a lot of great information for knitters, including knitting abbreviations, a needle conversion chart, articles about knitting machines and looms, and much more. Let's get started, and dive right into the world of knitting.

How to Read Knitting Patterns

Many of you are likely already experienced knitters. But, many may also be newbies to knitting. So, for all of you newbies, or even you experienced knitters who haven't knitted in a while and want to brush up, we want to explain how to read a knitting pattern. Once you get the hang of reading one pattern, you will have no problem with any other pattern, including complicated ones. Your pattern basically tells you everything you need to know about the project, including what you need and how to create it.

Start at the Start

It is not a good idea to just jump right into the pattern instructions. There may be some very important instructions that you need to follow before you start working the pattern. For instance, a certain pattern may require that you use a specific type of yarn. If you use something different, your piece may not turn out as you expected it to. So, with that in mind, let's take a look at each part of a knitting pattern.

Choosing Yarn – It is very important that you choose yarn that is appropriate for the pattern you are working on. For example, if you are making a dishcloth that requires a heavier worsted yarn, you don't want to use thinner baby yarn. Not only will it be the wrong texture, it will also be a lot smaller, because the heavier yarn gives fewer stitches per inch than the thinner yarn.

Choosing Needles – Next, you need to look at the pattern to see which needles you need to use for the project. Again, this is important because it will greatly affect the overall project if you are using the wrong needles. Larger needles will require fewer stitches per inch, while smaller needles give you more stitches, and smaller stitches.

Gauge Swatch – Even if you are using the recommended needles and yarn, it is still a good idea to knit a small test piece to make sure that the gauge is accurate. Cast on the amount of stitches that are recommended to make a four-inch section, and knit for about four inches. Then measure it against the size noted in the pattern.

Pre-Wash Instructions – You also need to see if the measurements noted in the pattern are pre-wash or after-wash. Knitted pieces often shrink in the wash, unless you have a drying rack that you can stretch them out on so they retain their original shape and size.

Follow the Instructions – It is important that you follow the instructions row by row. If you are a beginning knitter, it is a good idea to use stitch markers so you can keep track of the row you are working on, and what has already been done. It is even more important to keep track of the pattern if you are using a chart.

Understand the Abbreviations – Rather than write everything out, which would take forever to do, most patterns are written with abbreviations. You will need to get to know these abbreviations in order to understand the pattern. Refer to the "Knitting Abbreviations" section of this e-book for a full list of abbreviations and symbols.

Read the Chart Instructions – If there is a chart in the pattern, be sure to read the instructions with the chart. Here, you will find information about any symbols in the chart. Symbols may vary from pattern to pattern, which is why it is so important to read the chart instructions.

January

Brrrrr! The weather is cold, so it is the ideal time of year to make some extra scarves, mittens, and ear warmers. This month, you will find loads of patterns for these items, as well as patterns for dishcloths, children's items, and more. You will never be cold again once you have plenty of hand-made knitted items to keep you warm.

SIMPLE DISHCLOTH

Materials

Cotton, worsted weight yarn   Knitting needles size US 6

Directions

Row 1: Cast 4 stitches onto the needles.
Row 2: K1, repeat 3X, turn
Row 3: K2, YO, K to end of row, turn
Next rows: Repeat row 3 until you have at least 44 stitches on the needle.
Next row: K1, K2 tog, YO, K2 tog. Repeat to end of row.
Next rows: Repeat previous row until there are four stitches left. Cast off.

Photo for reference only: http://bit.ly/1Mf7BAJ

GARTER STITCH SCARF

Materials

1 large skein Red Heart yarn   Knitting needles size US 10

Directions

Row 1: Cast on enough stitches to make 10 inches
Row 2: Knit straight across the row, turn.
Rows 3-end: Repeat row 2.

Finishing

Add a fringe to each end of the scarf.

Photo for reference only: http://bit.ly/1TWZZuN

SIMPLE BABY BLANKET

Materials

2 balls soft baby yarn   Knitting needles size 10mm and 5.5mm

Directions

Row 1: Working with two strands of yarn and smaller needles, cast on 90 stitches.
Rows 2-6: Knit.
Rows 7-11: Switch to larger needles and knit.
Rows 12-16: Switch to smaller needles and knit.
Rows 17-end: Continue in this pattern, alternating needle sizes every five rows, until the piece is square. End with smaller needles.

Photo for reference only: http://bit.ly/1pn57f1

*E*ASIEST HAT PATTERN EVER **January 4**

Materials

1 skein Red Heart yarn
Knitting needles size 5.5 mm

Yarn needle

Directions

Row 1: Cast 78 stitches onto the needle.
Row 2: Knit.
Rows 3-end: Repeat row 2 until piece measures 10-12 inches. Cast off, and leave a long tail for stitching.

Finishing

Fold piece in half and stitch along the side. Loosely stitch across the top, pull the yarn tight, and bind off.

Photo for reference only: http://bit.ly/1Rfi5kQ

*E*ASY NECK WARMER **January 5**

Materials

1 skein Red Heart yarn
Knitting needles size 6.5mm

Yarn needle

Directions

Row 1: Cast 36 stitches onto needle.
Row 2: Knit.
Rows 3-end: Repeat row 2. Cast off.

Finishing

Photo for reference only: http://goo.gl/7ycQOi

*F*ASHION SCARF **January 6**

Materials

1 skein Red Heart yarn
Knitting needles size 5.5mm

2 stitch holders
Yarn needle

Directions

Row 1: Cast 28 stitches onto the needle.
Row 2: Knit.
Next rows: Continue knitting in garter stitch until piece measures 8 inches.

Next rows: Knit 14, put remaining stitches onto the stitch holder. Continue knitting the first 14 stitches for 5 inches. Place stitches onto a stitch holder, and knit the other section for 5 inches. Place all 28 stitches on the needle, and knit for 8 more inches.

Finishing

Add a fringe at each end of the scarf. The hole in the scarf is so you can put one end through and don't have to worry about tying it in a knot.

Photo for reference only: http://goo.gl/9OwkAa

HAND WARMERS   January 7

Materials

1 skein medium worsted weight yarn   Yarn needle
Knitting needles size US 8

Directions

Row 1: Cast 30 stitches onto needle.
Row 2: K1, P1 to end of row.
Row 3: Continue with K1, P1 (stockinette stitch) until piece measures 6.5 inches. Cast off and leave a tail for stitching.

Finishing

Fold piece in half lengthwise, and stitch along the side, leaving a gap for your thumb to fit through.

Photo for reference only: http://goo.gl/XlFwOv

DRAWSTRING PURSE   January 8

Materials

1 skein Red Heart worsted weight yarn   Yarn needle
Knitting needles size 7 mm   Crochet hook

Directions

Bottom of Bag

Row 1: Cast 12 stitches onto needle.
Row 2: Kfb, K to last stitch, Kfb.
Row 3: Knit.
Next rows: Repeat rows 2 and 3 until there are 26 stitches on the needle.
Next 10 rows: Knit.
Next row: K2tog, K to last 2 stitches, K2tog.
Next row: Knit.

Next rows: Continue working the previous two rows until you are back to having 12 stitches on the needle. Cast off and set piece aside.

Sides of Bag

Row 1: Cast 74 stitches onto the needle.
Rows 2-49: Knit.
Row 50: *K4, BO 1. Repeat from * to end of row.
Rows 51-56: Knit and cast off, leaving a long tail for stitching.

Finishing

Fold the main section of the bag in half lengthwise, and stitch along the side with the yarn needle. Pin this section to the bottom section, and stitch together. Crochet a chain to use as the drawstring for the bag, long enough to be a handle or a strap. Weave chain through the top section of the bag.

Photo for reference only: http://goo.gl/p7Q6VF

BATHROOM MAT   January 9

Materials

5 50g balls of worsted weight yarn   Knitting needles size 6mm

Directions

Row 1: Cast 75 stitches onto needle.
Row 2: K1, *P1, K1. Repeat from * to end of row.
Row 3: P1, *K1, P1. Repeat from * to end of row.
Row 4: Repeat row 3.
Row 5: Repeat row 4.
Next rows: Repeat rows 2-5 until piece reaches desired length. Cast off.

Photo for reference only: http://goo.gl/iNwBlD

SQUARE COASTERS   January 10

Materials

Scraps of worsted weight yarn   Knitting needles size 6.5mm

Directions

Row 1: Cast on 20 stitches.
Rows 2-21: Knit, cast off.

Photo for reference only: http://goo.gl/LiXaR5

Chunky Knit Scarf

Materials

2 skeins Red Heart worsted weight yarn   Yarn needle
Knitting needles size 15mm

Directions

Row 1: Using 2 strands of yarn, cast 15 stitches onto needle.
Rows 2-101: Knit. Cast off.

Finishing

Add a fringe to each end of the scarf.

Photo for reference only: http://goo.gl/PCFN5G

Knitting Needle Case

Materials

1 skein worsted weight yarn   Yarn needle
Knitting needles size 6mm   Crochet hook

Directions

Row 1: Cast 20 stitches onto the needle.
Next rows: K until piece is at least 2 inches longer than your knitting needles. Cast off.

Finishing

Fold piece in half lengthwise, and stitch along the side. With crochet hook, crochet a chain and weave it through the top of the bag to use as a drawstring.

Photo for reference only: http://goo.gl/cfl0p7

Ear Warmer

Materials

1 skein worsted weight yarn   Yarn needle
Knitting needles size 5mm   Crochet hook

Directions

Row 1: Cast 27 stitches onto the needle.
Row 2: Slip first stitch. K 25 stitches, P.
Row 3: Slip first stitch. K 26 stitches.
Rows 4-end: Repeat rows 2 and 3 until piece is long enough to fit comfortably around your head and cover your ears. Cast off and leave a tail long enough for stitching.

Finishing

Crochet a chain about 12-14" in length. Stitch up the ends of the knitted piece. Wrap the crochet chain around the stitched part a couple of times to cover the seam, and tie in a bow.

Photo for reference only: http://goo.gl/4GFLll

Warm Winter Scarf   January 14

Materials

3 skeins worsted weight yarn   Large yarn needle
Knitting needles size 15mm

Directions

Row 1: Knitting with three strands of yarn, cast 16 stitches onto the needle.
Row 2: Knit all the way across.
Row 4: Purl all the way across.
Rows 3-end: Repeat rows 2 and 3 until piece reaches desired length.

Finishing

Add a fringe to each end of the scarf.

Photo for reference only: http://goo.gl/K7FmTv

Easy Beanie Hat   January 15

Materials

1 skein worsted weight yarn   Yarn needle
Knitting needles size 5.5mm

Directions

Row 1: Cast 85 stitches onto the needle.
Row 2: Knit all the way across.
Row 3: Purl all the way across.
Rows 4-end: Repeat rows 2 and 3 until piece measures approximately 10". Cast off, leaving a tail for stitching.

Finishing

Fold the piece in half and stitch along the side. Loosely stitch along the top, and pull the yarn to gather the top of the hat and close the hole. Make a pompom, and attach to the top of the hat.

OWL HOOD   January 16

Materials

1 skein worsted weight yarn   Circular knitting needles size 5mm

Directions

Round 1: Cast 92 stitches onto the needle.

Rounds 2-end: Knit all the way around. Use a stitch marker to keep your place at the end of each round. Every few rounds, check to make sure that the work isn't twisting. Continue until pieces measures approximately 22". Cast off.

Photo for reference only: http://goo.gl/hj2mx7

*E*ASY FINGERLESS MITTENS   January 17

Materials

1 skein worsted weight yarn   Yarn needle
Knitting needles size 5mm

Directions

Make 2

Row 1: Cast 27 stitches onto the needle.

Row 2: Knit all the way across.

Rows 3-end: Repeat row 2 until piece is large enough to fit comfortably around your hand. Cast off and leave a tail for stitching.

Finishing

Fold each piece in half lengthwise, and stitch up the side, leaving plenty of space for your thumb.

Photo for reference only: http://goo.gl/guQwMV

OTHOLDER   January 18

Materials

1 skein worsted weight yarn   Crochet hook
Knitting needles size 5mm

Directions

Row 1: Cast 50 stitches onto the needle.

Row 2: Knit all the way across.

Rows 3-end: repeat row 2 until piece is a square. Cast off, leaving a long tail.

Finishing

Using the tail, crochet a chain measuring 4". Tie off, and stitch end of chain into beginning chain stitch.

Photo for reference only: http://goo.gl/Wj53Wj

CELL PHONE COZY January 19

Materials

1 skein worsted weight yarn
Knitting needles size 4.5mm

Yarn needle
Crochet hook

Directions

Row 1: Cast 8 stitches onto the needle.
Row 2: Knit all the way across.
Row 3: Purl all the way across.
Rows 4 to end: Repeat rows 2 and 3 until piece measures 7.5".
Next row: Decrease 1 stitch (hole for antenna), purl to end of row.
Next row: K4, K2tog, K1.
Next row: Repeat row 3.
Next row: K3, K2tog, K1.
Next row: Repeat row 3.
Next row: K2, K2tog, K1.
Next row: Repeat row 3.
Next row: K1, K2tog, K1. Cast off.

Finishing

Fold piece in half, and stitch side and bottom seams closed. Crochet a chain measuring 2-3", and attach at the top as a button loop. Stitch a button to the front of the cozy.

Photo for reference only: http://goo.gl/GZ4hrp

DOLL SLING January 20

Materials

1 skein worsted weight yarn

Knitting needles size 10mm

Directions

Row 1: Cast 24 stitches onto the needle.
Row 2: Knit all the way across.
Row 3: Repeat row 2 until piece measures 8".
Next row: Right side facing, Kfb1, *K1, M1. Repeat from * to end of row.
Next row: Purl all the way across.
Next row: Knit all the way across. Repeat last 2 rows for 8".

Next row: Right side facing, K2tog all the way across.

Next row: Purl all the way across.

Next row: Knit all the way across. Repeat last 2 rows until finished piece measures 25". Cast off.

Photo for reference only: http://goo.gl/p3TNYb

Ribbed Beanie   January 21

Materials

2 skeins worsted weight wool yarn   Yarn needle
Round knitting or double pointed needles
size 5mm

Directions

Round 1: With 2 strands of yarn together, cast 76 stitches onto the needle. Use a stitch marker to keep your place at the end of each round.

Round 2: Knit all the way around. Repeat until piece measures 10".

Next 2 rounds: K2tog all the way around.

Next round: K1. K2tog all the way around. Cut yarn and pull tail through stitches on the needle to close the hole. Weave end through and tie off.

Photo for reference only: http://goo.gl/y4fX3z

Potato Chip Scarf   January 22

Materials

1 skein Red Heart Boutique Sashay yarn   Needle and thread
Knitting needles size 5.5 mm

Directions

Row 1: Lay the yarn flat, and use the hole in the yarn as the actual yarn, so the rest is not knitted. About 4" in, begin casting on 6 stitches.

Row 2: Knit between the threads of the mesh all the way across.

Rows 3-end: Continue knitting until there is about a yard of yarn remaining. Bind off loosely.

Finishing

Tuck ends of scarf under, and stitch in place with the needle and thread to create a hem.

Photo for reference only: http://goo.gl/8Yuy5i

QUICK AND EASY COWL

Materials

3 skeins worsted weight yarn

Round knitting needle size 9mm

Directions

Round 1: Cast 62 stitches onto the needle.
Round 2: K1, *yo, K3tog, yo, K3. Repeat from * to the last 7 stitches, yo, K3tog, yo, K4.
Round 3: Knit all the way around.
Round 4: K4, *yo, K3tog, yo, K3. Repeat from * to the last 4 stitches, yo, K3tog, yo, K1.
Round 5: Repeat round 3.
Rounds 6-end: Repeat rounds 2-5 until piece measures 10-12", ending on a round 2 or round 4. Cast off.

Photo for reference only: https://goo.gl/mwX1gF

HOODED NEWBORN HAT

Materials

4 skeins worsted weight yarn
Knitting needles size 12mm

Yarn needle

Directions

Row 1: With 4 strands of yarn together, cast 10 stitches onto the needle.
Row 2: Knit all the way across.
Rows 3-end: Repeat row 2 until piece measures 12". Cast off, leaving a long tail for stitching.

Finishing

Stitch up the back of the hat. Make 3 tassels, and attach one at each end and at the top.

Photo for reference only: http://goo.gl/unw2Iw

COTTON FACECLOTH

Materials

1 skein cotton worsted weight yarn
Knitting needles size 4mm

Crochet hook or yarn needle

Directions

Row 1: Cast 48 stitches onto the needle.
Row 2: K3, P3. Repeat to end of row.
Rows 3-4: Repeat row 2.
Row 5: P3, K3. Repeat to end of row.
Row 6: Repeat row 2.

Rows 7-9: Repeat row 5.
Row 10: Repeat row 2.
Row 11: Repeat row 5.
Rows 12-end: Repeat rows 2-11 until piece measures 10". Cast off.

Photo for reference only: http://goo.gl/w4Wh0w

INFINITY SCARF   January 26

Materials

2 skeins worsted weight yarn   Circular knitting needle size 9mm

Directions

Row 1: With 2 strands of yarn together, cast 50 stitches onto the needle.
Rows 2-50: Knit all the way around, using a stitch marker to keep track of the rounds. Cast off.

Photo for reference only: http://goo.gl/1Rw8Bv

LACY SHAWL   January 27

Materials

1 skein Red Heart worsted weight yarn   Yarn needle
Knitting needles size 5mm

Directions

Row 1: Cast 5 stitches onto the needle.
Row 2: P1, *yo, P2tog. Repeat from * to end of row.
Row 3: Knit all the way across.
Row 4: K1, M1, K to last stitch, M1, K1.
Row 5: Repeat rows 2-4 until piece measures approximately 36 inches.
Last 4 rows: Knit all the way across, cast off.

Finishing

Add a fringe along the two shorter ends of the shawl.

Photo for reference only: http://goo.gl/9bNshr

KITTY TUNNEL   January 28

Materials

1 skein bulky yarn   Plastic tubing
Circular knitting needle or double pointed   Yarn needle
needles size 10mm

Directions

Round 1: Cast 90 stitches onto the needle. Use a stitch marker to keep track of the rounds.

Round 2: Knit all the way around. Continue knitting until piece reaches the desired length, plus 4". Cast off.

Finishing

Cut the plastic tubing so it will fit around each end of the knitted tube. Place tubing on the piece, leaving an inch of overhang. Fold the overhang over, and stitch it all the way around to secure the tubing. Repeat at the other end.

FLOOR MAT   January 29

Materials

6 skeins thick wool or bulky weight yarn   Knitting needles size 15mm

Directions

Row 1: Working with 2 strands of yarn, cast 50 stitches onto the needle.

Row 2: K1, P1. Repeat all the way to the end of the row.

Row 3: P over the K stitches, and vice versa to end of row.

Rows 4-end: Repeat rows 2 and 3 until piece reaches desired size. Cast off.

Photo for reference only: http://goo.gl/Oot9kv

BABY BLANKET   January 30

Materials

7 skeins of soft, worsted weight yarn   Yarn needle
Circular knitting needle size 5mm

Directions

Row 1: Cast 140 stitches onto the needle.

Next rows: Knit all the way across, turning for each row instead of working in rounds. Continue until the end of the skein.

Next rows: With second color, repeat first pattern. Continue doing this until you have used all of the colors, or as may colors as you want to have in the blanket. Cast off.

Photo for reference only: http://goo.gl/6IHGDz

Materials

2 twin bed sheets, ripped into strips that   Knitting needles size 16mm
  are 1.5" wide. Connect each strand with
  a tight knot.

Directions

Row 1: Cast 26 stitches onto the needle.

Row 2: Right side facing, *K1, P1. Repeat from * 4 times. P1, K8, P1. **P1, K1. Repeat from ** 4 times.

Row 3: *K1, P1. Repeat from * 4 times. K1, P8, K1. **P1, K1. Repeat from ** 4 times.

Row 4: Repeat row 2.

Row 5: Repeat row 3.

Row 6: Repeat row 2.

Row 7: Repeat row 3.

Row 8: Repeat row 2.

Row 9: Repeat row 3.

Rows 10-end: Repeat these 8 rows until piece reaches desired size. Cast off on row 2 of the pattern.

Photo for reference only: http://goo.gl/X1okTX

$\mathcal{K}$NITTING ABBREVIATIONS

This is going to be a long list, but don't get discouraged. You don't have to read it all now. It is here for you to reference as you are working on the patterns in this e-book. All terms are in alphabetical order, so you can find them easily if you are stuck while working on a pattern. There are some abbreviations used in knitting that are just symbols. These will be in a separate list following the alphabetical list.

Abbreviations in Alphabetical Order

alt – alternate
approx – approximately
beg – beginning
bet – between
BO – bind off
CA – color A
CB – color B
CC – contrasting color
cm – centimeters
cn – cable needle
CO – cast on
cont – continue
dec – decrease
dpn – double pointed needles
fl – front loop
foll – following
g – gram
inc – increase
k (K) – knit
k2tog – knit to stitches together (decrease)
kwise – knitwise
LH – left hand
lp(s) – loop(s)
m – meter
M1 – make one stitch
M1 p-st – make one purl stitch
MC – main color
mm – millimeter
oz – ounces
p (P) – purl
pat(s) – pattern(s)
pm – place marker
pop – popcorn

p2tog – purl two stitches together

prev - previous

psso – pass slipped stitch over

pwise – purlwise

rem – remaining

rep – repeat

rev ST st – reverse stockinette stitch

RH – right hand

rnd(s) – round(s)

RS – right side

sk – skip

skp – slip, knit, pass stitch over (decrease)

sk2p – slip 1, knit 2 together, pass slip stitch over knit 2 together (2 decreased stitches)

sl – slip

sl1k – slip 1 knitwise

sl1p – slip 1 purlwise

sl st – slip stitch

ssk – slip, slip, knit the two slip stitches together (decrease)

sssk – slip, slip, slip, knit the three slip stitches together

st(s) – stitch(es)

St st – stockinette or stocking stitch

tbl – through back loop

tog – together

WS – wrong side

wylb – with yarn in back

wyif – with yarn in front

yd(s) – yard(s)

yfwd – yarn forward

yo – yarn over

yrn – yarn around needle

yon – yarn over needle

Knitting Symbols

[] – Work the instructions inside the brackets the amount of times as per instructions

() – Work the instructions in the parenthesis in the area as per instructions

** - Repeat instructions following this symbol

* - Repeat instructions following this symbol as per instructions

" – Inches

February

It's still cold outside, so we are offering up a lot more easy to knit items for winter. Of course, Valentine's Day is this month, so we thought we'd throw in a chart. This will get you used to reading charts, and you can use the same chart for many of the Valentine's Day patterns. Don't forget to try the other patterns we have selected for this month. They are quick and easy to make up, and they are fun projects to create on cold winter nights.

UG COZY

Materials

1 skein Red Heart worsted weight yarn   Yarn needle
Knitting needles size 5mm

Directions

Row 1: Cast 34 stitches onto the needle.
Rows 2-6: K1, P1. Repeat pattern to end of row.
Row 7: Increase. *K1, P1. Repeat from * to last stitch, increase.
Row 8: Knit.
Row 9: Purl
Row 10: Knit
Row 11: Purl
Row 12: Right side facing, increase, knit to last stitch, increase.
Row 13: Purl
Rows 14-18: K1, P1. Repeat pattern to end of row. Cast off.

Finishing

Stitch up the seam to create a tube. If you want, stitch on some embellishments, such as buttons, rhinestones, etc.

Photo for reference only: http://goo.gl/gOHp7L

OGA MAT BAG

Materials

1 skein Red Heart worsted weight yarn   Crochet hook
Knitting needles sizes 5mm and 5.5m

Directions

Bag

Row 1: Cast 80 stitches onto the smaller needles.
Row 2: Purl across.
Row 3: K2, *yo, sl1, k2tog, psso, yo, k1. Repeat from * to the last 2 sts, k2.
Row 4: Purl across.
Row 5: K2, *k1, yo, sl1, k2tog, psso, yo. Repeat from * to the last 2 sts, k2.
Row 6: Purl across.
Row 7: K1, k2tog. *yo, k1, yo, sl1, k2tog, psso. Repeat from * to the last 5 sts, yo, k1, yo, ssk, k2.
Row 8: Purl across.
Next rows: Repeat rows 2-8 until piece measures about 15". Bind off.

Strap

Row 1: Working with 2 strands of yarn, cast 6 stitches onto larger needles
Row 2: K1, P1. Repeat pattern 3 times.
Rows 3-end: Repeat row 2 until strap measures 30". Bind off.
Drawstring
Crochet a chain measuring 24".

Finishing

Fold bag section in half lengthwise, and stitch along the side. Loosely stitch along the bottom edge, and pull tightly to close the hole. Stitch the strap to either end of the bag. Run the drawstring through the top edge of the bag.

Photo for reference only: http://goo.gl/JCk5FP

Baby Booties   February 3

Materials

1 skein worsted weight yarn   Yarn needle
Knitting needles size 5mm

Directions

Row 1: Cast 26 stitches onto the needle.
Rows 2-11: Knit all the way across.
Row 12: Bind off 10 stitches, knit to end of row.
Row 13: Bind off 10 stitches.
Rows 14-end: Knit remaining 6 stitches for 20 rows. Bind off.

Finishing

Lay piece out so it looks like a "T". Take the right arm and fold it so the bottom edge is flush with the bottom edge of the middle arm. Pin in place. Do the same with the left arm. Stitch this section together, and stitch along the sides. Turn right side out.

Photo for reference only: http://goo.gl/E0xP5Y

Heart Chart   February 4

Materials

Red and white worsted weight yarn
Knitting needles (any size, depending on the pattern you are using the chart in)

Directions

Row 1: With white yarn, cast on 15 stitches.
Row 2: Knit all the way across.
Row 3: Purl all the way across.

Row 4: K7 white, K1 red, K7 white.
Row 5: P6 white, P3 red, P6 white.
Row 6: K5 white, K5 red, K5 white.
Row 7: P4 white, P7 red, P4 white.
Row 8: K3 white, K9 red, K3 white.
Row 9: P2 white, P11 red, P2 white.
Row 10: K2 white, K11 red, K2 white.
Row 11: P2 white, P11 red, P2 white.
Row 12: K2 white, K11 red, K2 white.
Row 13: P2 white, P11 red, P2 white.
Row 14: K3 white, K4 red, K1 white, K4 red, K3 white.
Row 15: P4 white, P2 red, P3 white, P2 red, P4 white.
Row 16: Knit white all the way across.
Row 17: Purl white all the way across.

Photo for reference only: http://goo.gl/sTb8dy

HEART SCARF   February 5

Materials
1 skein each Red Heart white and red yarn
Knitting needles size 8mm

Directions
Row 1: Cast 30 stitches onto needle with white yarn.
Row 2: Knit all the way across.
Row 3: Purl all the way across.
Even rows: K15, follow pattern for heart chart rows 4-17.
Odd Rows: P15, follow pattern for heart chart rows 4-17.
Next rows: Repeat pattern, knitting the chart pattern first, followed by the white section. Continue alternating this pattern until piece reaches desired length. Bind off.

Finishing
Add a red and white fringe to each end of the scarf.

HEART PURSE   February 6

Materials
1 skein each red and white Red Heart worsted weight yarn
Knitting needles size 8mm
Yarn needle
Crochet hook

Red or white button
Needle and thread

Directions

Make 2 heart patches, following the directions for the heart chart.

With right sides facing each other, stitch the patches together along both sides and the bottom.

With 1 strand each of red and white yarn, crochet a chain measuring 36".

Attach chain to each side of the top of the purse.

Attach yarn at the top center of the back section, and crochet a chain measuring 3". Attach end of chain to beginning chain stitch to form a button loop.

Stitch button onto the front of the purse.

HEART PINCUSHION   February 7

Materials

Red and white Red Heart worsted weight yarn

Knitting needles size 6mm

Yarn needle

Fiberfill stuffing

Directions

Make a heart patch, following the directions for the heart chart.

Make a second patch all in white.

Finishing

With right sides facing, stitch pieces together all the way around, leaving a 2" opening on one side. Turn piece inside out, stuff with fiberfill, and stitch the opening shut.

HEART TOTE BAG   February 8

Materials

1 skein each red and white Red Heart worsted weight yarn

Knitting needle size 6mm

Yarn needle

Crochet hook

8" zipper

Needle and thread

Directions

Make 10 heart patches using the heart chart pattern.

Make 8 patches of the same size, using all red yarn.

Stitch patches together in the following formation:

Row 1 – 1 heart, 1 red, 1 heart

Row 2 – 1 red, 1 heart, 1 red

Row 2 – 1 heart, 1 red, 1 heart

Repeat for back section.

Finishing

With 4 strands of yarn (2 red, 2 white), crochet a chain measuring 42", leaving ends to look like a fringe.

Stitch front and back sections of bag together with front sides facing each other. Stitch along the bottom and both sides.

Attach crochet chain to each side at the top of the bag.

Stitch the zipper in at the top of the bag.

Photo for reference only: https://goo.gl/Ezt3Gu

Striped Scarf   February 9

Materials

3 skeins Red Heart yarn, different colors   Yarn needle
Circular knitting needle size 5.5mm

Directions

Row 1: Cast 241 stitches onto the needle.

Row 2: K1, P1. Repeat pattern to end of row.

Rows 3-end: Repeat row 2 for 8 rows. Change colors. Repeat pattern. Change colors. Continue changing colors until the scarf is the desired width. Bind off.

Finishing

Add a fringe to each end of the scarf.

Photo for reference only: http://goo.gl/YZGJKr

Striped Pot Holder   February 10

Materials

Worsted weight yarn in 3 colors   Crochet hook
Knitting needles size 8mm

Directions

Row 1: Working with 3 strands of 1 color, cast 17 stitches onto the needle.

Row 2: Right side facing, K1. *P1, K1. Repeat from * to end of row.

Rows 3-9: Repeat row 2. Switch to 3 strands of the next color.

Row 10: Knit all the way across.

Rows 11-13: Repeat row 2.

Rows 14-15: With next color, work stocking stitch.

Row 16: With second color, knit all the way across.

Rows 17-23: Repeat row 2. Bind off.

Finishing

Attach crochet hook at one corner of the pot holder, chain 10, attach chain at first chain stitch to create a loop for hanging.

Photo for reference only: http://goo.gl/ZckEhp

Heart Pot Holder   February 11

Materials

Red and white Red Heart worsted weight yarn

Knitting needles size 7mm
Crochet hook

Directions

Row 1: Cast 25 stitches onto the needle.
Row 2: Knit all the way across.
Row 3: Purl all the way across.
Rows 4-9: Repeat rows 2 and 3.
Row 10: K5, first row of heart chart, K5.
Odd Rows: P5, follow instructions for heart chart, P5.
Even rows: K5, follow instructions for heart chart, K5.
Final 10 rows: Knit one row, purl one row. Bind off.

Finishing

Attach crochet hook at one corner of the pot holder, chain 10, attach chain at first chain stitch to create a loop for hanging.

Heart Headband   February 12

Materials

Red and white Red Heart worsted weight yarn

Knitting needles size 6mm
Yarn needle

Directions

Row 1: Cast 27 stitches onto the needle.
Row 2: Knit all the way across.
Row 3: K10, first row of heart chart pattern, K10.
Row 4: P10, second row of heart chart pattern, P10.
Rows 5, 7, 9, 11, 13: K10, follow heart chart pattern, K10.
Rows 6, 8, 10, 12: P10, follow heart chart pattern, P10.
Row 13: Knit all the way across.
Row 14: Purl all the way across. Bind off.

Finishing

Fold in half with right sides facing each other. Stitch ends together, turn inside out to wear.

HEART COASTERS February 13

Materials
Red and white Red Heart worsted weight yarn
Knitting needles size 10mm

Directions
Follow the instructions for the heart chart.

HEART TIE BELT February 14

Materials
Red and white Red Heart worsted weight yarn

Circular knitting needle size 6mm or whatever size needed to get a gauge of 5 stitches per inch

Directions
Row 1: Cast on 270 stitches. You will be working back and forth and not in rounds.
Row 2: K15, follow row 1 of heart chart pattern 15 times, K15.
Row 3: P15, follow row 2 of heart chart pattern 15 times, P15.
Even rows: K15, follow heart chart pattern 15 times, K15.
Odd Rows: P15, follow heart chart pattern 15 times, P15. Bind off.

Finishing
Add a fringe to each end of the tie belt.

EASY INFINITY SCARF February 15

Materials
1 large skein worsted weight yarn

Circular knitting needle size 6mm

Directions
Round 1: Cast 200 stitches onto the needle.
Round 2: Knit all the way around.
Round 3: *K2, P2. Repeat from * all the way around.
Rounds 4: Repeat rounds 2 and 3 until piece measures 10".

Photo for reference only: http://goo.gl/Ly7xQd

INTER TOQUE

Materials

1 skein Red Heart worsted weight yarn   Yarn needle
Circular and double pointed knitting
needles size 9mm

Directions

Round 1: Cast 44 stitches onto the needle. Use a stitch marker to keep track of the rounds.

Round 2: Purl all the way around.

Round 3: Knit all the way around. Continue knitting until piece measures 7-8", or whatever length you need to fit. Switch to double pointed needles.

Next round: *K2, K2tog. Repeat from * to end of round.

Next round: Knit all the way around.

Next round: *K1, K2tog. Repeat from * to end of round.

Next round: Knit all the way around.

Next round: *K2tog. Repeat from * to end of round.

Next round: Knit all the way around.

Finishing

Pass the yarn needle through all of the stitches on the needle, and pull to close hole. Stich ends.

Photo for reference only:0020http://www.acraftyhouse.com/2011/11/that-favorite-winter-hat-pattern.html

SOFT BABY BLANKET

Materials

5 skeins soft, worsted weight yarn   Yarn needle
Circular knitting needle size 6.5mm

Directions

Row 1: Cast 5 stitches onto the needle. Work as if working with straight needles, back and forth.

Row 2: Knit all the way across.

Row 3: K3, yo, K2.

Row 4: K3, yo, K3.

Row 5: K3, yo, knit all the way across.

Next rows: Repeat row 5 until there are 154 stitches on the needle.

Next row: K2, K2tog, yo, K2tog, knit all the way across.

Next rows: Repeat last row until there are 5 stitches on the needle. Bing off.

Photo for reference only: http://goo.gl/oUx2S3

EASY BLANKET

Materials

2 skeins 5 weight yarn   Circular knitting needle size 10mm

Directions

Row 1: Cast 85 stitches onto the needle. Work as if working with straight needles, back and forth.
Rows 2-5: Knit all the way across.
Row 6: K5, *insert needle, yo twice, K1. Repeat from * to last 5 stitches, K5.
Row 7: Knit all the way across, working first loops for each stitch but dropping the extra loops.
Next rows: Repeat rows 6 and 7 until piece reaches desired length.
Last 4 rows: Knit all the way across. Bind off.

Photo for reference only: http://goo.gl/evYgHK

PRETTY VEST

Materials

2 skeins Red Heart worsted weight yarn   Yarn needle
Knitting needles size 4mm

Directions

Pattern written in size small. Medium, large, and extra-large sizes are in brackets.

Back

Row 1: Cast 94 (106, 116, 128) stitches onto the needle.
Row 2: Knit all the way across.
Row 3: Purl all the way across. Continue in a stocking stitch pattern until piece measures 15".
Next 4 rows (armhole): Continue working in stocking stitch. Bind off 8 stitches at the beginning of each row.
Next 2 rows: Continue working in stocking stitch. Bind off 7 stitches at the beginning of each row.
Next 8 rows: Continue working in stocking stitch.
Next rows: Continue working in stocking stitch. Increase 1 stitch at the beginning of first row, and then every fourth row, 9 (9, 9, 10) times. Continue working in stocking stitch until armhole measures 9" (9.5, 10, 11). End with right side facing, and bind off.

Left and Right Front

Row 1: Cast 52 (58, 63, 69) stitches onto the needle.
Row 2: Knit all the way across.
Row 3: Purl all the way across. Continue working in stocking stitch until piece measures 15", ending with right side facing.

Next rows (armhole): Bind off 5 (5, 6, 7) stitches at the beginning of the row. Continue working in stocking stitch. At the beginning of each of the next 8 (9, 9, 10) right side rows, decrease 1 stitch and continue working in stocking stitch until armhole measures 9" (9.5, 10, 11).

Next rows (shoulder and collar): Bind off 17 (22, 26, 30) stitches at the beginning of the next row. Knit to the end of the row. Continue knitting in stocking stitch for 3" (3.25, 3.5, 3.75), ending with right side facing. Bind off.

Finishing

Lay pieces out flat and stitch together with yarn needle.

Photo for reference only: http://goo.gl/di8OWQ

ONCHO SWEATER   February 20

Materials

8-12 balls super chunky yarn   Yarn needle
Knitting needles size 15mm

Directions

Pattern written in size small. Larger sizes are in brackets.

Front and back panels

Row 1: Cast 35 (37, 39, 41, 43) stitches onto the needle.
Row 2: Wrong side facing, knit all the way across.
Row 3: K2, yo, K2tog, K to last 4 stitches, k2tog, yo, k2.
Row 4: K2, P2. *K1, P1. Repeat from * to last 5 stitches. K1, P2, K2.
Next rows: Repeat rows 3 and 4 until piece measures 39.5" (41.5, 43.5, 45.5, 47.5).
Next row: Wrong side facing, knit all the way across. Bind off.

Finishing

Place panels on top of one another, wrong side out. Stitch shoulder seams across each side, leaving plenty of space for your head to go through. Stitch the bottom corners together for a batwing style sleeve.

Photo for reference only: http://goo.gl/8wC6or

NITTED NECKLACE   February 21

Materials

Any yarn (thicker is better)   Circular knitting needle size 8mm

Directions

Round 1: Cast 90-100 stitches onto the needle.
Rounds 2-8: Knit all the way around. Bind off.

Photo for reference only: http://goo.gl/INhl1S

KNITTED BRACELET

Materials

Any yarn (thicker is better)   Double pointed knitting needles size 8mm

Directions

Round 1: Cast on enough stitches to make 7.5 inches.
Rounds 2-8: Knit all the way around. Bind off.

"BEADED" NECKLACE

Materials

Worsted weight yarn   2 double pointed knitting needles size 4mm

Directions

Row 1: Cast 3 stitches onto the needle.
Row 2: Knit all the way across. Slide stitches onto the right-hand side of the needle, pull yarn tightly. Repeat until cord is the desired length.
Row 3: Right side facing, Kfb 3 times
Row 4: Purl all the way across.
Row 5: K1, kfb 4 times, k1.
Row 6: Purl all the way across.
Row 7: Knit all the way across.
Row 8: P1, P2tog 4 times, P1.
Row 9: K2tog 3 times. Tug the I-cord to make the edges roll inwards and create a "bead".
Next rows: Repeat row 2 for desired length.
Next rows: Repeat rows 3-9. Continue in cord and bead pattern until piece reaches desired length. Tie ends together and trim.

Photo for reference only: http://goo.gl/9uexbM

FUNKY CHUNKY HAT

Materials

Super Chunky Yarn
Double pointed knitting needles size 15mm

Directions

Round 1: Cast 18 stitches onto the needles.
Round 2: Knit all the way around. Use a stitch marker to keep track of rounds.
Rounds 3-11: Repeat round 2.

Round 12: K2tog all the way around. Pull yarn through remaining stitches and pull tight to close the hole.

Photo for reference only: http://goo.gl/VSURZC

Striped Blanket   February 25

Materials

7 skeins worsted weight yarn, different colors   Circular knitting needles size 6mm

Directions

Row 1: With first color, cast 150 stitches onto the needle. You will be working back and forth, and not in rounds.

Row 2: Knit all the way across.

Rows 3-end of skein: Repeat row 2. Switch colors and repeat. Continue with this pattern until all of the yarn has been used.

Photo for reference only: http://goo.gl/ZsUsNn

Warm Shawl   February 26

Materials

300 grams worsted weight yarn   Crochet hook
Circular knitting needle size 5mm

Directions

Row 1: Cast 3 stitches onto the needle.

Row 2: Knit all the way across.

Rows 3-6: Repeat row 2.

Row 7: Increase 1 stitch, K to last stitch, increase 1 stitch.

Row 8: Knit all the way across.

Rows 9-end: Repeat rows 7 and 8. Bind off.

Finishing

Using the crochet hook, add a fringe around the shorter ends of the shawl.

Photo for reference only: http://goo.gl/YFNylb

ℬULKY NECK WARMER

Materials

1 skein Red Heart Super Saver worsted weight yarn
Circular knitting needle size 5mm

Directions

Round 1: Cast 90 stitches onto the needle.
Round 2: Knit all the way around. Use a stitch marker to keep track of the beginning of each round.
Rounds 3-57: Repeat round 2. Bind off.

Photo for reference only: http://goo.gl/KsQ1we

ℬRIMMED HAT

Materials

1 skein chunky yarn   Circular knitting needle size 10mm

Directions

Pattern is for a child's hat. The adult size is in brackets.
Row 1: Cast 44 (48) stitches onto the needle.
Next rows: Knit all the way to end of row for 6 (10) rows.
Next row: Right side facing, K2tog all the way to end of row.
Next row: P2tog to end of row.
Next row: K2tog to end of row (one extra stitch remaining).
Next row: Bring yarn end through remaining stitches and tie off.

Photo for reference only: https://goo.gl/ULOJgk

ℛIBBED BRIM BEANIE

Materials

1 skein Red Heart Soft yarn   Double pointed knitting needles size 5mm
Circular knitting needles size 4.5mm and   Yarn needle
5mm

Directions

Round 1: With smaller circular needle, cast 100 stitches onto the needle. Join, and use a stitch marker to keep track of the beginning of each round.
Round 2: K2, P2 all the way around.
Next rounds: Repeat round 2 until piece measures 2".

Next rounds: Switch to larger circular needle, and knit each round until piece measures 7". Switch to double pointed needles to shape crown.

Round 1 of crown: K8, K2tog all the way around.

Round 2 of crown (and all even rounds): Knit all the way around.

Round 3: K7, K2tog all the way around.

Round 5: K6, K2tog all the way around.

Round 7: K5, K2tog all the way around.

Round 9: K4, K2tog all the way around.

Round 11: K3, K2tog all the way around.

Round 12: K2, K2tog all the way around.

Round 13: K1, K2tog all the way around.

Round 14: K2tog all the way around. Thread yarn through remaining stitches, pull tight, and tie off. Weave in ends.

Photo for reference only: http://goo.gl/FcAly3

$\boldsymbol{K}$NITTING NEEDLE CONVERSION CHART

Different parts of the world have different numbers and symbols for knitting needle sizes. So, if you are planning on starting a new pattern and you don't have the right needles, you will need to know all of the options available. The following is a knitting needle conversion chart that you should always keep handy. That way, you will never be wondering which needles to use, or trying to choose alternate needles that are not meant for the particular pattern you are working on because you don't know the conversions. The three main sizes for knitting needles are Metric, US, and Canadian/UK.

Conversion Chart

Metric (mm)	US	Canada/UK
2.0	0	14
2.25	1	13
2.75	2	12
3.0	-	11
3.25	3	10
3.5	4	-
3.75	5	9
4.0	6	8
4.5	7	7
5	8	6
5.5	9	5
6.0	10	4
6.5	10 ½	3
7	-	2
7.5	-	1
8.0	11	0
9.0	13	00
10.0	15	000
12.0	17	-
16.0	19	-
19.0	35	-
25.0	50	-

March

We celebrate St. Patrick's Day this month, so naturally we are offering a few shamrock patterns. This month is also devoted to special knitting stitches so you can create some amazing projects that people won't be able to believe you made yourself. You will find a great selection of specialty stitches, as well as a project to help you practice each stitch. Be sure to save all of your practice squares, because we have a pattern at the end of the year that puts all of those pieces together.

Diamond Brocade Stitch

Materials

Worsted weight yarn
Knitting needles for the pattern you are working on

Directions

Row 1: Cast 9 stitches onto the needle.
Row 2: Right side facing, K4. *P1, K7. Repeat from * to last 5 stitches, P1, K4.
Row 3: P3. *K1, P1, K1, P5. Repeat from * to last 6 stitches, K1, P1, K1, P3.
Row 4: K2. *P1, K3. Repeat from * to last 3 stitches, P1, K2.
Row 5: P1. *K1, P5, K1, P1. Repeat from * to end of row.
Row 6: *P1, K7. Repeat from * to last stitch, P1.
Row 7: Repeat row 5.
Row 8: Repeat row 4.
Row 9: Repeat row 3.

Photo for reference only: http://goo.gl/bjC4pN

Diamond Brocade Dishcloth

Materials

Worsted weight yarn   Knitting needles size 6mm

Directions

Row 1: Cast 54 stitches onto the needle.
Rows 2-end: Follow pattern for diamond brocade stitch all the way across each row. Bind off.

Chunky Winter Scarf

Materials

2-3 skeins chunky yarn   Knitting needles size 8mm

Directions

Row 1: Cast 24 stitches onto the needle.
Rows 2 to end: Knit all the way across. Bind off.

Finishing

Add fringes to each end of the scarf.

NITTING A CABLE STITCH March 5

Materials

Worsted weight yarn
Knitting needles needed for pattern you are working on

Directions

Row 1: Cast 14 stitches onto the needle.
Row 2: P4, K6, P4
Row 3: K4, P6, K4
Row 4: P4, K6, P4
Row 5: K4, P6, K4
Row 6: P4, sl 3 stitches to CN and hold in front, K3 from LH needle, K3 from CN, P4.
Row 7: K4, P6, K4
Next rows: Repeat rows 2-7.

Photo for reference only: http://goo.gl/dAWj1e

CABLE STITCH SCARF March 6

Materials

2 skeins Red Heart Super Saver yarn   Knitting needles size 6mm

Directions

Row 1: Cast 56 stitches onto the needle.
Next Rows: Work cable stitch pattern 4 times. Repeat until piece reaches desired length.

Finishing

Add fringes to each end of the scarf.

KNITTING A BASKET WEAVE STITCH March 7

Materials

Worsted weight yarn
Knitting needles for the pattern you are using

Directions

Row 1: Cast 13 stitches onto the needle.
Row 2: Knit all the way across.
Row 3: K5. *P3, K5. Repeat from * to end of row.
Row 4: P5. *K3, P5. Repeat from * to end of row.
Row 5: Repeat row 3.

Row 6: Repeat row 4.
Row 7: K1, P3. *K5, P3. Repeat from * to end of row.
Row 8: P1, K3. *P5, K3. Repeat from * to end of row.
Row 9: Repeat row 7.

Photo for reference only: http://goo.gl/rmtx1Y

$\mathcal{B}$ASKET STITCH SCARF March 8

Materials

2 skeins Red Heart Super Saver yarn   Knitting needles size 6mm

Directions

Row 1: Knit all the way across.
Rows 2-9: Follow pattern for basket stitch. Continue following this pattern until piece reaches desired length.
Last row: Knit all the way across.

Finishing

Add fringes to each end of the scarf.

$\mathcal{K}$NITTING A RIPPLE STITCH March 9

Materials

Worsted weight yarn
Knitting needles for the pattern you are using

Directions

Row 1: Cast 14 stitches onto the needle.
Row 2: K6. *P2, K6. Repeat from * to end of row.
Row 3: K1. *P4, K4. Repeat from * to last 5 stitches, P4, K1.
Row 4: P2. *K2, P2. Repeat from * to end of row.
Row 5: P1. *K4, P4. Repeat from * to last 5 stitches, K4, P1.
Row 6: K2. *P2, K6. Repeat from * to last 4 stitches, P2 K2.
Row 7: P6. *K2, P6. Repeat from * to end of row.
Row 8: P1. *K4, P4. Repeat from * to last 5 stitches, K4, P1.
Row 9: K2. *P2, K2. Repeat from * to end of row.
Row 10: K1. *P4, K4. Repeat from * to last 5 stitches, P4, K1.
Row 11: P2. *K2, P6. Repeat from * to last 4 stitches, K2, P2.

Photo for reference only: http://goo.gl/fVlzNc

RIPPLE STITCH SCARF

Materials

2 skeins Red Heart Super Saver Yarn   Knitting needles size 6mm

Directions

Row 1: Cast 56 stitches onto the needle.
Rows 2-11: Follow the ripple stitch pattern.
Next rows: Continue with the ripple stitch pattern until piece reaches desired length.

Finishing

Add fringes to each end of the scarf.

KNITTING A CHEVRON STITCH

Materials

Worsted weight yarn   Knitting needles for the project you are working on

Directions

Row 1: Cast 15 stitches onto the needle.
Row 2: K1, K2tog. *K4, dbl inc, K4, dbl dec. Repeat from * to last 3 stitches, ssk, K1.
Row 3: Purl all the way across.
Rows 4-end: Repeat rows 2 and 3.

Photo for reference only: http://goo.gl/drV4gS

CHEVRON BABY BLANKET

Materials

6 balls Red Heart Soft Baby Steps yarn
(use 1 or more colors depending on your
skill level)

Circular knitting needle size 5.5mm
Yarn needle

Directions

Row 1: Cast 150 stitches onto the needle. Work as with regular needles and not in rounds.
Rows 2-6: Knit all the way across.
Row 7: Knit all the way across.
Row 8: Purl all the way across.
Row 9: K3. *(K2tog) twice, (yo, K1) 4 times, (K2tog) twice. Repeat from * to last 3 stitches, K3.
Row 10: Knit all the way across.
Rows 11-14: Repeat rows 7-10 until piece reaches desired length.

Rows 15-19: Knit all the way across. Bind off.

Photo for reference only: http://goo.gl/Ihb67N

KNITTING **D**IAGONAL **R**IBBING   March 13

Materials

Worsted weight yarn   Needles for the project you are working on

Directions

Row 1: Cast 14 stitches onto the needle.
Row 2: K1, P4. *K4, P4. Repeat from * to last stitch, K1.
Row 3: K4. *P4, K4. Repeat from * to last 2 stitches, P2.
Row 4: K3. *P4, K4. Repeat from * to last 3 stitches, P3.
Row 5: K2, P4. *K4, P4. Repeat from * to end of row.
Row 6: P1. *K4, P4. Repeat from * to last 5 stitches, K4, P1.
Row 7: P4. *K4, P4. Repeat from * to last 2 stitches, K2.
Row 8: P3. *K3, P4. Repeat from * to last 3 stitches, K3.
Row 9: P2. *K4, P4. Repeat from * to last 4 stitches, K4.
Next rows: Repeat rows 2-9 to create pattern

Photo for reference only: http://goo.gl/FzG0hM

GREEN **D**IAGONAL **R**IBBING **W**ASHCLOTH   March 14

Materials

Green cotton worsted weight yarn   Knitting needles size 7mm

Directions

Row 1: Cast 56 stitches onto the needle.
Row 2: Follow rows 2-9 of diagonal ribbing pattern. Repeat until piece is a square. Bind off.

KNITTING A **B**OX **S**TITCH   March 15

Materials

Worsted weight yarn
Knitting needles for the pattern you are working on

Directions

Row 1: Cast 14 stitches onto the needle.
Rows 2 and 5: *K2, P2. Repeat from * to last 2 stitches, K2.
Row 3 and 4: *P2, K2. Repeat from * to last 2 stitches, P2. Repeat rounds 2-5 to complete pattern.

Photo for reference only: http://goo.gl/0vnter

*B*ox Stitch Emerald Shoulder Bag **March 16**

Materials

1 skein emerald green Red Heart Super
Saver Yarn
Knitting needles size 6.5mm
Yarn needle

Large and small crochet hooks
Button (emerald gemstone)
Needle and thread

Directions

Row 1: Cast 56 stitches onto the needle.

Next rows: Follow box stitch pattern until piece measures 16".

Next rows: Continue following the box stitch pattern, but decrease one stitch at each end of each row until there is 1 stitch remaining. Bind off.

Finishing

With crochet hook and 5 strands of yarn together, crochet a chain measuring 36". Fold knitted piece so the bottom edge lines up with the beginning of the decrease section. Stitch along each side. Stitch the strap to either side of the top of the purse. At the center point of the flap, using the smaller hook, crochet a chain of 6 stitches, and attach at the first chain. Tie off. Fold the flap over, and stitch a button onto the front of the purse where the button loop lays.

*K*nitting Textured Stripes **March 17**

Materials

Worsted weight yarn
Knitting needles for the project you are working on

Directions

Row 1: Cast 15 stitches onto the needle.

Rows 2, 4, and 7: Knit all the way across.

Rows 3, 5, and 6: Purl all the way across. Repeat rows 2-7 to complete pattern.

Photo for reference only: http://goo.gl/Nz0WCs

*T*extured St. Patty's Day Stripes Blanket **March 18**

Materials

1 skein each green and 1 variegated
green Red Heart Super Saver Yarn
Circular knitting needle size 8mm

Directions

Row 1: Knit back and forth instead of working in rounds. Cast 200 stitches onto the needle.

Next rows: Follow the pattern for the textured stripes until piece measures 5". Switch colors.

Next rows: Follow the pattern for the textured stripes until piece measures 10". Switch colors. Continue following striping pattern until piece reaches desired length. Bind off.

Finishing

Add a fringe all the way around the blanket.

KNITTING AN OPEN CABLE STITCH   March 19

Materials

Worsted weight yarn

Knitting needles for the project you are working on

Directions

Row 1: Cast 11 stitches onto the needle.

Rows 2 and 4: Wrong side facing, K3, P2, K1, P2, K3.

Row 3: P3, sl next 3 stitches to cn (1 P st and 2 K st) and hold back, sl next p st back to LH needle, p, K2 from cn, P3.

Row 5: P2, back cross, P1, front cross, P2.

Row 6: K2, P2, K3, P2, K2.

Row 7: P1, back cross, P3, front cross, P2.

Rows 8 and 10: K1, P2, K5, P2, K1.

Row 9: P1, K2, P5, K2, P1.

Row 11: P1, front cross, P3, back cross, P1.

Row 12: K2, P2, K3, P2, K2.

Row 13: P2, front cross, P1, back cross, P2. Repeat rows 2-13 to create pattern.

Photo for reference only: http://goo.gl/BpNTwi

OPEN CABLE STITCH SCARF   March 20

Materials

1 skein Red Heart Super Saver Yarn

Knitting needles size 6mm

Directions

Row 1: Cast 66 stitches onto the needle.

Next rows: Follow pattern for open cable stitch until piece reaches desired length. Bind off.

Finishing

Add a fringe to each end of the scarf.

Knitting Faggot Lace Patterns

Materials

Worsted weight yarn
Knitting needles for the pattern you are working on

Directions

Row 1: Cast 20 stitches onto the needle.
Row 2: K1. *yo, P2tog. Repeat from * to last stitch, K1. Repeat this row over and over to create pattern.

Photo for reference only: http://goo.gl/HCJPN0

Faggot Stitch Wrap

Materials

2 skeins Red Heart Super Saver Yarn   Knitting needles size 8mm

Directions

Row 1: Cast 70 stitches onto the needle.
Row 2: Work Faggot stitch pattern until piece measures 48". Bind off.

Finishing

Add a fringe to each of the short sides, and one of the long sides.

Knitting a Moss Stitch

Materials

Worsted weight yarn
Knitting needles for the project you are working on

Directions

Row 1: Cast 21 stitches onto the needle.
Rows 2 and 5: K1. *P1, K1. Repeat from * to end of row.
Rows 3 and 4: P1. *K1, P1. Repeat from * to end of row. Continue repeating rows 2-5 to create pattern.

Photo for reference only: http://goo.gl/4z7QW6

Moss Stitch Lap Blanket

Materials

3-4 skeins Red Heart Super Saver   Circular knitting needle size 6mm
worsted weight yarn

Directions

Row 1: Work back and forth and not in the round. Cast 145 stitches onto the needle.

Next rows: Follow the pattern for knitting a moss stitch until piece measures desired length. Bind off.

Photo for reference only: http://goo.gl/7ZCXtL

*K*NITTING A HALF LINEN STITCH   March 25

Materials

Worsted weight yarn
Knitting needles for the project you are working on.

Directions

Row 1: Cast 15 stitches onto the needle.
Row 2: Purl all the way across.
Row 3: *K1, yarn forward, sl 1 stitch purlwise, yarn back. Repeat from * to last stitch, K1.
Row 4: Purl all the way across.
Row 5: *K2, yarn forward, sl 1 stitch, yarn back, K1. Repeat from * to last stitch, K1.
Row 6: Purl all the way across. Repeat rows 2-6 to create pattern.

Photo for reference only: http://goo.gl/OAQHCu

*H*ALF LINEN STITCH COWL   March 26

Materials

2 colors Red Heart Super Saver worsted weight yarn
Circular knitting needles size 5.5mm

Directions

Round 1: Cast 99 stitches onto the needle with main color. Use a stitch marker to keep track of the beginning of each round.
Round 2: Purl all the way around.
Round 3: K1. *Slip 1 stitch with yarn in front, K1. Repeat from * to end of round.
Round 4: Knit all the way around.
Round 5: Slip 1. *K1, slip 1 stitch with yarn in front. Repeat from* to end of round.
Round 6: Knit all the way around. Switch colors.
Next rounds: Repeat rows 2-6 in second color. Switch colors. Continue in this pattern until piece measures 8". Bind off.

Photo for reference only: http://goo.gl/PM4eDX

KNITTING A BROKEN RIB STITCH March 27

Materials

Worsted weight yarn
Knitting needles for the project you are working on

Directions

Row 1: Cast 14 stitches onto the needle.
Row 2: *K2, P2. Repeat from * to last 2 stitches, K2.
Row 3: Purl all the way across.
Next rows: Repeat rows 2 and 3 to create the pattern.

Photo for reference only: http://goo.gl/CdYGbD

BROKEN RIB STITCH HAT March 28

Materials

1 skein Red Heart Super Saver worsted weight yarn

Circular and double pointed knitting needles size 4mm

Directions

Round 1: Cast 88 stitches onto the needle.
Round 2: *K2, P2. Repeat from * to end of row.
Next rounds: Repeat row 2 until piece measures 1 ¼".
Next 2 rounds: Knit all the way around.
Next 2 rounds: *K2, P2. Repeat from * to end of round.
Next rounds: Repeat last 4 rounds until piece measures 5 ½".
Next round: *K6, K2tog. Repeat from * to end of round.
Next round: Knit all the way around.
Next round: *K2, P2tog, K2, P1. Repeat from * to end of round.
Next round: *K2, P1. Repeat from * to end of round.
Next round: *K4, ssk. Repeat from * to end of round.
Next round: *K3, ssk. Repeat from * to end of round.
Next round: *K2, P2. Repeat from * to end of round.
Next round: *K2, P2tog. Repeat from * to end of round.
Next round: *K1, ssk. Repeat from * to end of round.
Next round: SSK to end of round.
Next round: K1. *ssk. Repeat from * to end of round. Pull yarn through remaining stitches and weave in ends.

Photo for reference only: http://goo.gl/JA9XxW

KNITTING FEATHER AND FAN LACE

Materials

Worsted weight yarn
Knitting needles for the pattern you are working on

Directions

Row 1: Cast 22 stitches onto the needle.
Row 2: Knit all the way across.
Row 3: Purl all the way across.
Row 4: *K2tog, K2tog, yo, K1, yo, K1, yo, K1, yo, K2tog, K2tog. Repeat from * to end of row.
Row 5: Knit all the way across. Repeat rows 2-5 to create pattern.

Photo for reference only: http://goo.gl/q3JQyp

FEATHER AND FAN LACE BABY BLANKET

Materials

2-3 skeins soft worsted weight yarn   Circular knitting needles size 6.5mm

Directions

Row 1: Work back and forth and not in rounds. Cast 155 stitches onto the needle.
Row 2: Knit all the way across.
Row 3: Purl all the way across.
Row 4: *K2tog, K2tog, yo, K1, yo, K1, yo, K1, yo, K2tog, K2tog. Repeat from * to end of row.
Row 5: Knit all the way across. Repeat rows 2-5 to create pattern, and until pieces reaches desired size. Bind off.

Photo for reference only: https://goo.gl/38FVby

BLOCKED INFINITY SCARF

Materials

Scraps of worsted weight yarn (this is a   Knitting needles size 5mm
scrap buster project)   Yarn needle

Directions

Row 1: Cast 50 stitches onto the needle.
Row 2: Knit all the way across. Continue knitting, changing colors as you run out of scraps. Knit until piece measures 78". Bind off.

Finishing

Fold piece in half, and stitch short ends together.

Photo for reference only: http://goo.gl/qNrR76

HOW TO USE A KNITTING CHART

If you are going to be putting a design with different colors, or you are going to be knitting lace, you will need to know how to read knitting charts. They are also used for many cable knit patterns. Basically, the purpose of these charts is to have a visual guide that eliminates the need for additional written instructions. If there are any special stitch instructions within the chart, they will be noted in the actual pattern.

Don't be afraid to use charts. They are really easy to use, and once you start, you will likely catch on right away. Basically, it is a picture of the design, broken down into little squares. Each square represents a stitch. Inside each square, you will see a color designation. Often, these charts are in color, so you can easily see what the abbreviations for the colors mean.

Reading a Chart

All work on knitting charts start at the bottom right-hand corner of the chart. You will be working across each row on the chart, from right to left. So, when you are working on the front, you will be working from right to left. When you are working on the opposite side, you will be working those rows on the chart backwards. If you are working with round needles, you will not be switching sides. Instead, use stitch markers to indicate the beginning and end of the chart section of the pattern. Work from right to left of the chart for each round.

Charts have numbers to designate the stitch number, as well as the row that you are working on. If you are working on a flat piece, the numbers will be on each side of the chart. If you are working in the round, the numbers will only be on the right side of the chart in most cases.

Types of Knitting Charts

There are several different types of charts for a variety of knitting projects. The main charts you will be using in this e-book are stitch pattern charts and color knitting charts for patterns that involve alternating colors. Because there isn't a lot of space in charts, you will find that they have a lot of symbols and abbreviations. You can easily find all of the symbols and abbreviations in the "Knitting Abbreviations" section of this e-book.

April

Spring has sprung! It's time to spend your days outside, enjoying the sunshine. But, the nights are still chilly, so you have plenty of time to work on some fun knitting projects. This month, we are featuring patterns for Easter projects, as well as spring bonnets for babies, purses, and more. There are even a few patterns for cleaning items so you can get started on your spring cleaning (if you can put down your knitting long enough).

SCRAP YARN BLANKET

April 1

Materials

Small balls of scrap yarn

Circular knitting needle size 10mm

Directions

Row 1: Cast 200 stitches onto the needle.
Row 2: Knit all the way around.
Row 3: Purl all the way around.
Next rows: Repeat rows 2 and 3 until piece reaches desired length. When you run out of one color of yarn, join the next one and keep going. Bind off when finished.

Finishing

Add a fringe all the way around the blanket.

REMOTE CONTROL CADDY

April 2

Materials

1 skein Red Heart Super Saver worsted weight yarn

Knitting needles size 6mm or size to achieve a gauge of 5 stitches per inch
Yarn needle

Directions

Row 1: Cast 50 stitches onto the needle.
Row 2: Knit all the way across.
Row 3: Purl all the way across.
Next rows: Continue working in stockinette stitch until piece measures 24". Bind off.

Finishing

Fold piece at the 10" mark, and stitch along the sides. Stitch seams in this large pocket to create smaller pockets.

Photo for reference only: http://goo.gl/kTmhG9

STRIPED DISHCLOTH

April 3

Materials

3 skeins Red Heart Super Saver worsted weight yarn, different colors

Knitting needles size 7mm

Directions

Row 1: Cast 40 stitches onto the needle with Color A.

Row 2: Knit all the way across.
Row 3: Repeat row 2.
Next 2 rows: Repeat rows 2 and 3 with Color B.
Next 2 rows: Repeat rows 2 and 3 with Color C. Repeat striping pattern until piece is a square. Bind off.

Photo for reference only: https://goo.gl/3V43oP

SPRING FEATHER AND FAN STITCH SCARF April 4

Materials

2-3 skeins silky yarn   Knitting needles size 6mm

Directions

Row 1: Cast 22 stitches onto the needle.
Row 2: Knit all the way across.
Row 3: Purl all the way across.
Row 4: *K2tog, K2tog, yo, K1, yo, K1, yo, K1, yo, K2tog, K2tog. Repeat from * to end of row.
Row 5: Knit all the way across. Repeat rows 2-5 to create pattern until piece reaches desired length.
Next row: Purl all the way across.
Next row: Knit all the way across. Bind off.

Finishing

Add a fringe to each end of the scarf.

Photo for reference only: https://goo.gl/m0Wyjp

PENCIL CASE April 5

Materials

1 skein Red Heart Super Saver worsted   Yarn needle
   weight yarn   10-12" zipper
Knitting needles size 4.5mm   Needle and thread

Directions

Row 1: Cast 55 stitches onto the needle.
Row 2: Knit all the way across.
Row 3: Purl all the way across.
Next rows: Repeat rows 2 and 3 until piece measures 12". Bind off.

Finishing

Fold piece in half with wrong side facing, and stitch along the side seams with yarn and yarn needle. With the needle and thread, sew in the zipper along the top opening. Turn right side out.

Photo for reference only: http://goo.gl/7zA8oW

MUG COZY

Materials

1 skein chunky yarn
Knitting needles size 6.5mm

Yarn needle

Directions

Row 1: Cast 30 stitches onto the needle.
Row 2: Knit all the way across.
Row 3: Purl all the way across.
Next rows: Repeat rows 2 and 3 until piece measures is 3-3.5 inches long, or long enough to fit your favorite coffee mug. Bind off.

Finishing

Fold piece in half, and stitch up 3-4 stitches from the bottom, and the same at the top. This way, the cozy will stay on the mug, but the handle will be accessible.

DOLL BLANKET

Materials

1 skein pink Red Heart Super Saver
worsted weight yarn

Knitting needles size 6mm
Pink 1/2" satin ribbon

Directions

Row 1: Cast 3 stitches onto the needle.
Row 2: Knit all the way across, and for every row in pattern.
Next rows: Increase 1 stitch at the beginning of each row until piece measures 14".
Next rows: Decrease 1 stitch at the beginning of each row until 3 stitches remain. Bind off.

Finishing

Weave the ribbon all the way around the edge of the blanket, tie in a bow.

Photo for reference only: http://goo.gl/6p5S2w

SOAP SACHET BAG

Materials

1 ball worsted weight yarn
Knitting needles size 6mm

Crochet hook

Directions

Row 1: Cast 15 stitches onto the needle.
Rows 2-6: Knit all the way across.

Row 7: Purl all the way across.

Rows 8-end: Repeat rows 6 and 7 until piece measures 10". Bind off.

Finishing

Crochet a chain measuring 10". Fold knitted piece in half, and stitch up each side. Weave the crochet chain through the top garter stitch section of the sachet bag.

Photo for reference only: http://goo.gl/azXwz8

Easter Egg Hot Pad   April 9

Materials

Cotton yarn   Knitting needles size 5mm

Directions

Row 1: With 3 strands of yarn together, cast 6 stitches onto the needle.
Row 2: Knit all the way across.
Rows 3, 5, 7, 9, 11, and 13: Repeat row 2.
Rows 4, 6, 8, 10, 12, and 14: Kfb, knit to last stitch, kfb.
Rows 15-19: Knit all the way across.
Row 20: Kfb, knit to last stitch, kfb.
Row 21: Knit all the way across.
Row 22: Kfb, knit to last stitch, kfb.
Rows 23-25: Knit all the way across.
Row 26: Kfb, knit to last stitch, kfb.
Rows 27-33: Knit all the way across.
Row 34: K2tog, knit to end of row.
Rows 35-46: K2tog, knit to end of row.
Row 47: K2tog, K, K2tog, K, K2tog, K, K2tog. Bind off.

Photo for reference only: http://goo.gl/DF4FZ0

Easter Bunny Newborn Hat   April 10

Materials

1 skein Red Heart Super Saver worsted   Knitting needles size 6mm
weight yarn   Yarn needle

Directions

Hat Section

Row 1: Cast 48 stitches onto the needle.
Row 2: Knit all the way across.
Row 3: Purl all the way across.

Next rows: Work in stockinette stitch until piece measures 6", ending on a wrong side row.

Next row: *K2, K2tog. Repeat from * to end of row.

Next row: Purl all the way across.

Next row: *K1, K2tog. Repeat from * to end of row.

Next row: Purl all the way across.

Next row: K2tog all the way across. Pull yarn through remaining stitches and pull tight. Stitch along the side seam.

Ears (make 2)

Row 1: Cast 4 stitches onto the needle.

Row 2: K1, KFB, KFB, K1.

Row 3: Purl all the way across.

Row 4: K2, KFB, KFB, K2.

Row 5: Purl all the way across.

Rows 6-11: Work in even stockinette stitch.

Row 12: K2tog, K6, SKP.

Rows 13, 15, and 17: Purl all the way across.

Row 14: K2tog, K4, SKP.

Row 16: K2tog, K2, SKP.

Row 18: K2tog, SKP.

Row 10: P2tog. Bind off.

Finishing

Stitch ears to the top of the hat.

Photo for reference only: http://goo.gl/6EfOMj

Mini Stuffed Easter Eggs April 11

Materials

Worsted weight yarn

Double pointed knitting needles size 5mm

Yarn needle or crochet hook

Fiberfill stuffing

Directions

Round 1: Cast 8 stitches onto the needle.

Round 2: *K1, KFB. Repeat from * to end of round.

Round 3: *K2, KFB. Repeat from * to end of round.

Round 4: *K3, KFB. Repeat from * to end of round.

Round 5: Knit all the way around.

Round 6: *K4, KFB. Repeat from * to end of round.

Rounds 7-11: Knit all the way around.

Round 12: *K4, K2tog. Repeat from * to end of round.

Round 13: Knit all the way around.

Round 14: *K3, K2tog. Repeat from * to end of round.

Round 15: Knit all the way around.
Round 16: *K2, K2tog. Repeat from * to end of round.
Round 17: Knit all the way around.
Round 18: *K1, K2tog. Repeat from * to end of round.

Finishing

Stuff egg, then draw yarn through remaining stitches and pull tightly to close hole. Stitch with yarn needle or crochet hook.

Photo for reference only: http://goo.gl/uBnz4p

EASTER EGG BASKET   April 12

Materials

Worsted weight yarn   Yarn needle
Knitting needles size 4mm

Directions

Base

Row 1: Cast 25 stitches onto the needle.
Rows 2 and 3: Knit all the way across.
Row 4: K1. *P4, K4. Repeat from * to end of row.
Row 5: *K4, P4. Repeat from * to last stitch, K1.
Rows 6 and 7: Repeat row 5.
Rows 8 and 9: Knit all the way across. Bind off.

Main Section

Row 1: Cast 25 stitches onto the needle.
Row 2: Knit all the way across.
Next rows: Work basket stitch for 8 rows
Next row: *K3, K2tog. Repeat from * to end of row.
Next row: Knit all the way across.
Next row: *K2, K2tog. Repeat from * to end of row.
Next row: Knit all the way across.
Next row: *K1, K2tog. Repeat from * to end of row. Bind off.

Handle

Row 1: Cast 30 stitches onto the needle.
Rows 2, 3, and 4: Knit all the way across. Bind off.

Finishing

Fold main section in half and stitch along the side seam. Stitch main section to the base. Stitch handle to either side of the main section. Turn right side out.

Photo for reference only: http://goo.gl/X1hJwp

TEA POT COZY

Materials

Worsted weight yarn

Knitting needles size 6mm

Directions

Make 2 squares

Row 1: Cast 40 stitches onto the needle.
Row 2: Knit all the way across.
Next rows: Repeat row 2 until piece is a square. Bind off.

Finishing

Place both squares together back to back. Stitch 1/3 of the way up each side from the bottom, and from the top. Leave the center of each side open for the spout and handle to fit through. Crochet a chain measuring 12". Weave the chain through the top of the tea cozy, draw shut, and tie in a bow.

Photo for reference only: http://goo.gl/orR4PI

WINE SACK

Materials

1 skein Red Heart Super Saver worsted weight yarn

Double pointed knitting needles size 5mm
Crochet hook

Directions

Round 1: Cast 42 stitches over three needles.
Round 2: Wrong side facing, knit all the way around.
Round 3: Purl all the way around.
Round 4: Knit all the way around.
Round 5: Purl all the way around.
Round 6: Knit all the way around.
Next rounds: Knit all the way around until piece measures 17".
Next round: *K5, K2tog. Repeat from * to end of round.
Next round, and every second round: Knit all the way across.
Next round: *K4, K2tog. Repeat from * to end of round.
Next round: *K3, K2tog. Repeat from * to end of round.
Next round: *K2, K2tog. Repeat from * to end of round.
Next round: *K1, K2tog. Repeat form * to end of round.
Next round: K2tog all the way around.
Next round: Knit all the way around. Bind off.

Finishing

Crochet a chain measuring 12". Weave through the top section, and tie in a bow.

Photo for reference only: http://goo.gl/2ayW31

Ribbed Dishcloth April 15

Materials

Cotton worsted weight yarn   Knitting needles size 4.5mm

Directions

Row 1: Cast 45 stitches onto the needle.
Row 2: K3. *P1, K3. Repeat from * to end of row.
Row 3: Knit all the way across.
Next rows: Repeat rows 2 and 3 until piece measures about 10". Bind off.

Photo for reference only: http://goo.gl/CT1Bzn

Textured Dishcloth April 16

Materials

Cotton worsted weight yarn   Knitting needles size 4.5mm

Directions

Row 1: Cast 45 stitches onto the needle.
Row 2: Knit all the way across.
Row 3: K4, P34, K4.
Row 4: K4, P5. *K4, P6. Repeat from * 6 times, K4, P5, K4.
Row 5: K4, P34, K4.
Row 6: Knit all the way across.
Row 7: K4, P34, K4.
Row 8: K8. *P6, K4. Repeat from * 3 times, K4.
Row 9: K4, P34, K4.
Next rows: Repeat rows 2-9 until piece measures about 10". End with a knit row. Bind off.

Photo for reference only: http://goo.gl/8HSpsX

Multi-Colored Dishcloth April 17

Materials

Variegated cotton worsted weight yarn
Knitting needles size 4.5mm

Directions

Row 1: Cast 45 stitches onto the needle.
Row 2: *K1, P1. Repeat from * to end of row.
Next rows: Repeat row 2 until piece measures about 10". Bind off.

Photo for reference only: http://goo.gl/Ut4KAu

Toy Storage Hammock

Materials

2 skeins Red Heart Super Saver worsted weight yarn

Knitting needles size 5mm
Crochet hook

Directions

Row 1: Cast 160 stitches onto the needle.
Row 2: Wrong side facing, knit all the way across.
Row 3: K1, ssk. *Yo, K2tog. Repeat from * to last 3 stitches, K2tog, K1.
Row 4: Purl all the way across.
Row 5: K1, ssk. *ssk, yo. Repeat from * to last 3 stitches, K2tog, K1.
Next rows: Repeat rows 2-5 until 6 stitches remain on the needle.
Next row: K1, ssk, K2tog, K1.
Next row: Purl all the way across. Bind off.

Finishing

With the crochet hook, make chain loops and stitch to each corner of the toy hammock.

Photo for reference only: https://goo.gl/2JUUt3

Baby Doll

Materials

Sport weight yarn, pink and white
Knitting needles size 5mm
Crochet hook
Pink and white lace

Fiberfill stuffing
Needle and thread
Yarn needle
Buttons or felt for eyes

Directions

Row 1: Cast 16 stitches onto the needle with pink yarn.
Row 2: Increase all the way across (32 stitches).
Row 3: Purl all the way across.
Row 4: Knit all the way across.
Next rows: Work in stockinette stitch for 30 rows.
Next row (neck): K2tog all the way across.

Next row: Purl all the way across.

Next row (Head): Switch to white yarn. *K1, increase. Repeat from * to end of row.

Next rows: Work 12 rows in stockinette stitch.

Next row: Decrease 5 stitches evenly across row.

Next row: Purl all the way across.

Next row: K2tog all the way across. Bind off and leave a long tail for stitching.

Finishing

Pull yarn tight to close top of head. Stuff head, and stitch the back seam. Stuff the body, and stitch the back seam. Sew buttons or felt onto the face for eyes and other facial features. Sew lace around the top of the head to resemble a bonnet.

Photo for reference only: http://goo.gl/Yq0JJk

Door Draft Stopper   April 20

Materials

1 skein Red Heart Super Saver worsted weight yarn
Knitting needles size 4mm

Fiberfill stuffing
Yarn needle

Directions

Row 1: Cast 50 stitches onto the needle.

Row 2: Knit all the way across.

Row 3: Purl all the way across.

Next rows: Continue working in stockinette stitch until piece measures about 32". Bind off.

Finishing

Fold piece in half lengthwise, and stitch along one end. Gather the stitches at one end and pull tightly to close the opening. Stuff draft stopper, and repeat stitching the opposite end.

Photo for reference only: http://goo.gl/JyHldZ

Baby Bib   April 21

Materials

Worsted weight yarn
Knitting needles size 4.5mm

Circular knitting needle size 4.5mm

Directions

Round 1: With circular needle, cast on 60 stitches.

Round 2: *K2, P2. Repeat to end of round.

Next rounds: Repeat row 2 until piece measures 2".

Next round: Bind off 28 stitches, knit to end of round.

Next row: Switch to straight needles. Sl purlwise, K2, P to last 3 stitches, K2, P1.

Next row: Sl knitwise, knit to end of row.

Next row: Repeat last 2 rows until piece measures 8" from edge, ending with the wrong side facing.

Next row: Sl knitwise, K2, ssk, K to last 5 stitches, K2tog, K3.

Next row: Sl purlwise, K2, purl to last 3 stitches, K2, P1.

Next row: Sl knitwise, K2, ssk, K to last 5 stitches, K2tog, K3.

Next row: Sl purlwise, K2, ssk K to last 5 stitches, K2tog, K2, P1.

Next row: Sl knitwise, K2, ssk, K to last 5 stitches, K2tog, K3.

Next row: Sl purlwise, K2, ssk, K to last 5 stitches, K2tog, K2, P1. Bind off.

Photo for reference only: http://goo.gl/AD6j4g

NEWBORN MITTENS   April 22

Materials

Worsted weight yarn   Yarn needle
Knitting needles sizes 3.25mm and 4mm

Directions

Make 2

Row 1: Cast 30 stitches onto the needle.

Row 2: K2. *P2, K2. Repeat from * to end of row.

Row 3: P2. *K2, P2. Repeat from * to end of row.

Rows 4-21: Repeat rows 2 and 3.

Row 22: Repeat row 2.

Row 23: Repeat row 3, decreasing 1 stitch.

Row 24: K2tog tbl, K10, K2tog, K1, K2tog tbl, K10, K2tog.

Row 25: Purl all the way across.

Row 26: K2tog tbl, K8, K2tog, K1, K2tog tbl, K8, K2tog.

Row 27: Purl all the way across.

Row 28: K2tog tbl, K6, K2tog, K1, K2tog tbl, K6, K2tog.

Row 29: Purl all the way across. Bind off.

Finishing

Stitch top and side seam, and fold back the cuff.

Photo for reference only: http://goo.gl/fGMoeb

EWBORN SKIRT

April 23

Materials

Red Heart bulky yarn
Circular knitting needles sizes 6mm and 8mm

Directions

Round 1: Cast 50 stitches onto the smaller needle.
Round 2: *K2, P2. Repeat from * to end of round.
Rounds 3-7: Repeat round 2.
Rounds 8-27: Switch to larger needles. Knit all the way around. Bind off.

Photo for reference only: http://goo.gl/5snmYM

WAFFLE DISHCLOTH

April 24

Materials

Cotton worsted weight yarn   Knitting needles size 4mm

Directions

Row 1: Cast 30 stitches onto the needle.
Row 2: *K2, P2. Repeat from * to last 2 stitches, K2.
Row 3: *P2, K2. Repeat from * to last 2 stitches, P2.
Row 4: Knit all the way across.
Row 5: Purl all the way across.
Next rows: Repeat rows 2-6 until piece is a square, repeat rows 2 and 3 once more. Cast off in purl stitches.

Photo for reference only: http://goo.gl/fjQ88D

WARM BABY BLANKET

April 25

Materials

Chunky yarn   Circular knitting needle size 10mm

Directions

Row 1: Work back and forth and not in rounds. Cast 61 stitches onto the needle.
Row 2: *K1, P1. Repeat from * to end of row.
Next rows: Repeat row 2 until piece reaches desired size. Bind off.

Photo for reference only: http://goo.gl/m6u0d6

Change Purse

Worsted weight yarn

Knitting needles size 4.5mm

Button

Yarn needle

Needle and thread

Directions

Row 1: Cast 18 stitches onto the needle.

Row 2: Wrong side facing, knit all the way across.

Next rows: Work in stockinette stitch for 13 rows.

Next row: Wrong side facing, knit all the way across (turning row).

Next rows: Work in stockinette stitch for 19 rows.

Next row: Wrong side facing, knit all the way across (turning row).

Next rows: Work 2 rows in stockinette stitch.

Next row (right side): K1, skp, K to last 3 stitches, K2tog, K1.

Next row (wrong side): Purl all the way across.

Next right side rows: Repeat first right side row.

Next wrong side rows: Repeat first wrong side row.

Next row: P4, yo, P4 (9 stitches, buttonhole row)

Next row: Pearl all the way across.

Next row (right side): Work the first right side row. Bind off.

Finishing

Fold piece so flap folds over. Whip stitch sides together, and whip stitch around button hole to secure it. Sew a button onto the front with a needle and thread.

Photo for reference only: http://goo.gl/YpPyTx

Basket Stitch Placemat

Materials

Worsted weight yarn

Knitting needles size 6.5mm

Directions

Row 1: Cast 60 stitches onto the needle.

Row 2: Knit all the way across.

Next rows: Follow basket weave stitch until piece measures 14".

Next row: Knit all the way across. Bind off.

Photo for reference only: http://goo.gl/vSn8Tu

SIMPLE PLACEMAT April 28

Materials

Worsted weight yarn   Knitting needles size 6mm

Directions

Row 1: Cast 70 stitches onto the needle.
Row 2: Knit all the way across.
Next rows: Continue working in garter stitch until piece measures 14". Bind off.

Photo for reference only: https://goo.gl/KMLveb

SIMPLE COASTERS April 29

Materials

Worsted weight yarn   Knitting needles size 6mm

Directions

Row 1: Cast 20 stitches onto the needle.
Row 2: Kinit all the way across.
Next rows: Continue working in garter stitch until piece is square. Bind off.

Photo for reference only: https://goo.gl/hhRboJ

KITCHEN TOWEL April 30

Materials

1 skein cotton worsted weight yarn   Knitting needles size 7mm

Directions

Row 1: Cast 60 stitches onto the needle.
Rows 2-5: Knit all the way across.
Row 6: K4, P to last 4 stitches, K4.
Row 7: Knit all the way across.
Next rows: Repeat rows 6 and 7 until piece measures 22".
Next rows: Knit all the way across for 4 rows. Bind off.

Photo for reference only: https://goo.gl/EKakBu

How to Make Your Own Knitting Charts, the Old-Fashioned Way

Even though you are likely to never run out of knitting charts to work with, it may be that you can't find a chart with a design that you would really like to do. Don't worry, because it is super-easy to make your own knitting charts, and you don't need to go out and buy special computer software to do it. Sometimes, it is just as easy, and just as fast, to do things the old-fashioned way. So, with that in mind, we are going to tell you how to make your own knitting charts, the old-fashioned way.

One of the best things about making your own knitting charts is the fact that the items you make will be truly unique. They will be of your own design, and you will be that much more proud of the finished projects. You will need four things to create your knitting charts:

- A picture or an idea
- Knitter's graph paper
- Pencil
- Eraser

It doesn't get much more low-tech than this. All you have to do is draw your idea onto the knitter's graph paper, which you can find at the back of many pattern books, or available for download online. If it is a color pattern, color it in with colored pencils. Once you have the entire image complete, all you have to do is mark the stitch and row numbers along the sides of the chart. It's as simple as that. You can also go high-tech, and get software that will create the charts from scanned images. That just doesn't seem like it would be as much fun, for some reason.

Each time you create your own knitting chart, be sure to knit up a quick sample of the design to make sure that it works in a knitting pattern. There may be a bit of trial and error at first, but it won't be long before you are an expert at making your own knitting charts, the old-fashioned way.

May

Now that the weather is getting warmer, you are probably spending a lot more time outside. One way to enjoy the nice weather is to bring your knitting outside with you. Just think of how relaxing it will be to sit on your deck with a cup of coffee (or maybe a glass of wine), knitting and just enjoying the surroundings. We have plenty of patterns this month that can made up in a few hours, so they are perfect for making on these lazy spring days. This month's patterns include purses, belts, bow ties, and more.

SLOUCHY HAT

Materials

1 skein chunky yarn
Circular knitting needles size 8mm and 9mm
3 double pointed knitting needles size 9mm

Directions

Round 1: Cast 48 stitches onto the needle with smaller needle.

Round 2: *K2, P2. Repeat all the way around.

Next rounds: Repeat round 2 until piece measures 1.5". Switch to larger needle.

Next round: Knit all the way around.

Next round: Purl all the way around.

Next rounds: Repeat last 2 rounds until piece measures 8".

Next round: *K6, K2tog. Repeat from * to end of round.

Next round: Purl all the way around.

Next round: *K5, K2tog. Repeat from * to end of round.

Next round: Purl all the way around.

Next round: *K4, K2tog. Repeat from * to end of round.

Next round: Purl all the way around.

Next round: *K3, K2tog. Repeat from * to end of round.

Next round: Purl all the way around.

Next round: *K2, K2tog. Repeat from * to end of round. Pull yarn through remaining stitches to close opening. Tie off.

Photo for reference only: http://goo.gl/ZyxKkm

PONCHO

Materials

2 skeins Red Heart Super Saver worsted weight yarn
Circular knitting needles size 5.5mm

Directions

Round 1: Cast 316 stitches onto the needle. Place a stitch marker between stitches 158 and 159.

Round 2: With right side facing, K2. *YO, K2tog. Repeat from * to stitch marker. YO, remove stitch marker, K2, YO. **K2tog, YO. Repeat from ** to last 2 stitches, YO, K2.

Round 3: Knit all the way around.

Round 4: K2, SKP, K to 3rd stitch before 2 center stitches, SL1, K2tog, PSSO, YO K2, YO, K3tog, K to last 4 stitches, K2tog, K2.

Round 5: K2, P2tog, P to last 4 stitches, SSPtb (slip, slip, purl through back loops), K2.

Next rounds: Repeat rounds 4 and 5 until there are 12 stitches remaining.

Next row: With right side facing, K2, (SL1, K1, PSSO) twice, (K2tog) twice, K2.
Next row: K2, P2, SSptb, K2. Bind off.

Finishing

Knit eyelet lace edging all the way around the bottom of the poncho.

Lacy Wrap   May 3

Materials

1 skein Red Heart Super Saver worsted weight yarn
Knitting needles size 6.5mm

Directions

Special stitch: PSSO. Pass slipped stitch over. Insert left needle in the front of a slipped stitch, passing it over the stitch that was previously knit, yarn over and off needle.
Row 1: Cast 45 stitches loosely onto the needle.
Row 2: With right side facing, K1. *YO SL1, K1, YO, PSSO. Repeat from * to end of row.
Row 3: *P2, drop YO. Repeat from * to last stitch, K1.
Row 4: K2. *YO, SL1, K1, YO, PSSO. Repeat from * to last stitch, K1.
Row 5: P3. *Drop YO, P2. Repeat from * to end of row. Bind off.

Photo for reference only: http://goo.gl/oseIxY

Simple Wrap   May 4

Materials

2 skeins Red Heart Super Saver worsted weight yarn
Knitting needles size 6mm

Directions

Row 1: Cast 80 stitches onto the needle.
Next rows: Knit all the way across. Repeat until piece measures 4".
Next row: K3. *K1, YO, K2tog from back. Repeat from * to last 2 stitches, K2.
Next row: K4, YO, K2tog from back. *K1, YO, K2tog from back. Repeat from * to last 2 stitches, K2.
Next rows: Repeat last 2 rows until patterned section measures 4".
Next rows: Knit all the way across until section measures 4".
Next rows: Repeat last 2 sections until piece reaches desired length, ending on a knit section. Bind off.

Finishing

Add a fringe to each end of the wrap.

Photo for reference only: http://goo.gl/2vyr2Y

LIGHTWEIGHT SPRING SHAWL

Materials

2 skeins worsted weight chenille yarn   Circular knitting needle size 10mm

Directions

Special stitch: Wrap and turn. Yarn in front, SL1 to right needle, yarn between needles to back, SL stitch back to left needle. Turn work and bring yarn back to the opposite side between needles.

Row 1: Work back and forth instead of in rounds. Cast 150 stitches onto the needle.

Rows 2-3: Knit all the way across.

Row 4: K147, wrap and turn. Place marker on stitch 147.

Row 5: K144, wrap and turn. Place marker on stitch 144.

Rows 6-55: Work garter stitch, stopping 3 stitches before the end of the marker on each row.

Row 56: Knit to the end of the row, increase at marked stitches by 1 stitch. Take out the markers.

Row 57: K100 to middle of row. K to end of row, increasing by 1 stitch at each marked stitch. Take out the markers.

Row 58: Knit to the end of the row. Bind off.

Finishing

Add a fringe along the shorter sides of shawl.

Photo for reference only: http://goo.gl/OiNMds

ROUND DISHCLOTH

Materials

Worsted weight yarn
3 double pointed knitting needles size 4.5mm

Directions

Round 1: Cast 8 stitches onto the needles. Place a stitch marker at the first stitch.

Round 2: Knit through the back loop of each stitch to the end of row.

Round 3: *Yfwd, K1. Repeat from * 8 times.

Round 4 and all even rounds: Knit all the way around.

Round 5: *Yfwd, K2. Repeat from * 8 times.

Round 7: *Yfwd, K3. Repeat from * 8 times.

Round 9: *Yfwd, K4. Repeat from * 8 times.

Round 11: *Yfwd, K5. Repeat from * 8 times.

Round 13: *Yfwd, K6. Repeat from * 8 times.

Round 15: *Yfwd, K7. Repeat from * 8 times.

Round 17: *Yfwd, K8. Repeat from * 8 times.

Round 19: *Yfwd, K1, Yfwd, K2tog, K6. Repeat from * 8 times.

Round 21: *Yfwd, K1, (Yfwd, K2tog) twice, K5. Repeat from * to end of round.

Round 23: *Yfwd, K1, (Yfwd, K2tog) 3 times, K4. Repeat from * to end of round.
Round 25: *Yfwd, K1, (Yfwd, K2tog) 4 times, K3. Repeat from * to end of round.
Round 27: *Yfwd, K1, (Yfwd, K2tog) 5 times, K2. Repeat from * to end of round.
Round 29: *Yfwd, K1, (Yfwd, K2tog) 6 times, K1. Repeat from * to end of round.
Round 31: *Yfwd, K1, (Yfwd, K2tog) 7 times. Repeat from * to end of round.
Round 32: Purl all the way around.
Round 33: *INC 1 stitch in next stitch knitwise, K15. Repeat from * 8 times. Cast off purlwise.

Photo for reference only: http://goo.gl/Gh0u5G

SCRUBBING DISHCLOTH   May 7

Materials

1 skein Red Heart Scrubby yarn   Knitting needles size 5mm

Directions

Row 1: Cast on 30 stitches.
Next rows: Knit all the way across. Repeat until piece measures 8". Bind off.

Photo for reference only: http://goo.gl/Im3rHJ

RAINBOW DISHCLOTH   May 8

Materials

1 skein white worsted weight yarn
1 skein variegated worsted weight yarn
Knitting needles size 5mm

Directions

Row 1: Cast 45 stitches onto the needle with white yarn (main color).
Row 2: Knit all the way across.
Row 3: Attach color B, K4. *SL1P, K5. Repeat from * to last 5 stitches. SL1P, K4.
Row 4: With color B, K4. *YF, SL1P, YB, K5. Repeat from * to last 5 stitches, YF, SL1P, YB, K4.
Rows 5-6: Repeat rows 3 and 4.
Rows 7-8: With main color, knit all the way across.
Row 9: With color B, K1. *SL1P, K5. Repeat from * to last 2 stitches, SL1P, K1.
Row 10: With color B, K1. *YF, SL1P, YB, K5. Repeat from * to last 2 stitches, YF, SL1P, YB, K1.
Rows 11-12: Repeat rows 9 and 10.
Row 13: With main color, knit.
Next rows: Repeat rows 2-13 5 times. Bind off.

Photo for reference only: http://goo.gl/J5BwL9

TEXTURED STRIPES DISHCLOTH

May 9

Materials

Cotton worsted weight yarn   Knitting needles size 5mm

Directions

Special stitch: Tweed stitch (TS). Insert needle into a stitch 2 rows beneath, pull up a loop, K1, pass loop over stitch knitted.

Row 1: Cast 45 stitches onto the needle.
Row 2: K3. *K3, TS. Repeat from * to last 6 stitches, K6.
Rows 3 and all right side rows: K3, P to last 3 stitches, K3.
Row 4: K4. *TS, K3. Repeat from * to last 5 stitches, K5.
Row 6: Repeat row 2.
Row 8: Repeat row 4.
Row 10: Repeat row 2.
Row 12: Repeat row 4.
Row 13: Repeat row 3.
Next rows: Repeat rows 2-13 until piece is square. Bind off.

Photo for reference only: http://goo.gl/DSF2cM

STRAIGHT NEEDLE HAT

May 10

Materials

1 skein Red Heart Super Saver worsted weight yarn   Knitting needles size 5mm
Yarn needle

Directions

Row 1: Cast 103 stitches onto the needle.
Row 2: *K1, P1. Repeat from * to last stitch, K1.
Row 3: *P1, K1. Repeat from * to last stitch, P1.
Next rows: Repeat rows 2 and 3 until piece measures 8".
Next row: *(K1, P1) 11 times, K1, S2KP2, (K1, P1) 4 times. Repeat from * to last stitch, K1.
Next row: PL. *(K1, P1) 4 times, K1, S2KP2, (K1, P1) 11 times. Repeat from * to end of row.
Next row: *(K1, P1) 3 times, K3tog P1, (K1, P1) 6 times, S2KP2, P1, (K1, P1) 3 times. Repeat from * to last stitch, K1.
Next row: P1. *K1, P1. Repeat from * to end of row.
Next row: *(K1, P1) 2 times, K1, S2KP2, (K1, P1) 3 times. Repeat from * to last stitch, K1.
Next row: P1. *(K1, P1) 3 times, P2, (K1, P1) 2 times. Repeat from * to end of row.
Next row: *(K1, P1) 2 times, S2KP2, P1, (K1, P1) 2 times. Repeat from * to last stitch, K1.
Next row: P1. *K1, P1. Repeat from * to end of row.
Next row: *K1, P1, K1, S2KP2, (K1, P1, 2 times. Repeat from * to last stitch, K1.

Next row: P1. *K1, P1, S2KP2, P1, K1, P1. Repeat from * to end of row.
Next row: *K1, P1, S2KP2, P1, K1, P1. Repeat from * to last stitch, K1.
Next row: P1. *K1, P1. Repeat from * to end of row.
Next row: *K1m S2KP2, K1, P1. Repeat from * to last stitch, K1.
Next row: P1. *K1, P3. Repeat from * to end of row.
Next row: *S2KP2, P1. Repeat from * to last stitch, K1. Pull yarn through stitches, pull tight to close opening. Tie off.

Photo for reference only: http://goo.gl/tmhZYL

*B*ASKET WEAVE HAT May 11

Materials

1 skein Red Heart sparkle yarn   Yarn needle
Circular knitting needle size 4.5mm

Directions

Row 1: Work back and forth and not in rounds. Cast 91 stitches onto the needle.
Row 2: *K1, P1. Repeat from * to end of row.
Row 3: *P1, K1. Repeat from * to end of row.
Next rows: Repeat rows 2 and 3 until piece measures 1".
Next row: Knit all the way across, increasing 5 stitches across row.
Next row: Purl all the way across.
Basket weave row 1: With right side facing, *K3, P2. Repeat from * to last stitch, K1.
Row 2: Knit all the way across.
Row 3: *K1, P1, K1, P2. Repeat from * to last stitch, K1.
Row 4: Purl all the way across.
Row 5: *K2, P1, K1, P1. Repeat from * to last stitch, P1.
Row 6: Knit all the way across.
Next rows: Repeat basket weave rows 1-6 until piece measures 9", ending on row 6.
Crown row 1: *K3, P2tog. Repeat from * to last stitch, K1.
Row 2: Knit all the way across.
Row 3: *K2, P2tog. Repeat from * to last stitch, K1.
Row 4: Repeat crown row 2.
Row 5: *K1, P2tog. Repeat from * to last stitch, K1.
Row 6: Repeat row 2.
Row 7: *P2tog. Repeat from * to last stitch, K1. Pull yarn tightly through remaining stitches twice.

Finishing

Stitch seam together.

Photo for reference only:
http://www.allfreeknitting.com/Knit-Hats/Basketweave-Sparkle-Knit-Beanie-Pattern-From-Red-Heart

CHEVRON DISHCLOTH May 12

Special stitch: Crazy chevron.

Row 1: *KFB, K3, CDD, K2, KFB, K8, CDD, K7, KFB. Repeat from * to last 11 stitches, KFB, K3, CDD, K2.

Row 2: K1. *K9, P21. Repeat from * to last 10 stitches, K10.

Materials

Cotton worsted weight yarn, 3 colors   Knitting needles size 4.5mm and 5mm

Directions

Row 1: Cast 71 stitches onto the needle with color A.
Row 2: Knit all the way across.
Rows 3-17: Work crazy chevron pattern.
Rows 18-21: Work crazy chevron pattern in color B.
Rows 22-25: Work crazy chevron pattern in color C.
Rows 26-29: Work crazy chevron pattern in color B.
Rows 29-46: Work crazy chevron pattern in color A.
Rows 47-50: Work crazy chevron pattern in color B.
Rows 51-61: Work crazy chevron pattern in color A.
Row 62: Knit all the way across. Bind off.

Photo for reference only: http://goo.gl/oj3Q0G

CHENILLE SCARF May 13

Materials

2 skeins chenille worsted weight yarn   Knitting needles size 5.5mm

Directions

Row 1: Cast 40 stitches onto the needle.
Row 2: *K2, P2. Repeat from * to end of row.
Next rows: Repeat row 2 until piece reaches desired length. Bind off.

Photo for reference only: http://goo.gl/vLzO6y

FUZZY SCARF May 14

Materials

2-3 skeins fuzzy worsted weight yarn   Knitting needles size 6mm

Directions

Row 1: Cast 45 stitches onto the needle.

Row 2: Knit all the way across.

Next rows: Repeat row 2 until piece reaches desired length. Bind off.

Photo for reference only: http://goo.gl/YXsdMA

*L*ACE SHRUG

Materials

4 ounces fingering yarn   Yarn needle
Knitting needles size 2.75mm and 3.5mm   Crochet hook

Directions

Row 1: Cast 80 stitches onto the smaller needle.

Row 2: *K1, P1. Repeat from * to end of row.

Next rows: Repeat row 2 until piece measures 2".

Next row: Repeat row 2, increasing 32 stitches evenly across row.

Pattern row 1: Switch to larger needles. With right side facing, *K3, K2tog, YO, K1, YO, SL1, K1, pull slipped stitch over K stitch. Repeat from * to end of row.

Row 2: Purl all the way across.

Row 3: K2. *K2tog, YO, K3, YO, SL1, K1, pull slipped stitch over K stitch, K1. Repeat from * to last 4 stitches, YO, K4.

Row 4: Purl all the way across.

Row 5: K4. *YO, SL1, K2tog, pull slipped stitch over K stitch, YO, K5. Repeat from * to last stitch, YO, K1.

Row 6: Purl all the way across.

Row 7: Knit all the way across.

Row 8: Purl all the way across.

Next rows: Repeat pattern rows 1-8 until piece measures 29" above the ribbing.

Next row: Switch to smaller needles. Knit a rib stitch to end of row, decreasing 32 stitches evenly across row.

Next rows: Rib stitch for 2". Bind off.

Finishing

Fold piece in half lengthwise, stitch side seams 5.5". Single crochet all the way around.

Photo for reference only: http://goo.gl/EOeGJx

*B*ULKY YARN HAT

Materials

1 skein super chunky yarn
Circular knitting needle size 15mm
Yarn needle

Directions

Round 1: Cast 36 stitches onto the needle.

Round 2: Knit all the way around.

Rounds 3-16: Repeat round 2.

Round 17: *K4, K2tog. Repeat from * to end of round.

Round 18 and all even rounds: Knit all the way around.

Round 19: *K3, K2tog. Repeat from * to end of round.

Round 21: *K2, K2tog. Repeat from * to end of round.

Round 23: K2tog all the way around. Pull yarn through remaining stitches tightly to close opening. Fasten off.

Photo for reference only: http://goo.gl/c3FJG1

Ribbed Cowl May 17

Materials

1 skein Red Heart Soft yarn
Circular knitting needle size 5mm

Yarn needle

Directions

Round 1: Cast 120 stitches onto the needle.

Round 2: *K4, P4. Repeat from * to end of round.

Next rounds: Repeat round 2 until piece measures 10". Bind off.

Photo for reference only: http://goo.gl/oduWWT

Hooded Cowl May 18

Materials

1 skein Red Heart Super Saver worsted weight yarn
Circular knitting needle size 9mm

Directions

Round 1: Working with 2 strands of yarn, cast 100 stitches loosely onto the needle.

Round 2: *K5, P5. Repeat from * to end of round.

Round 3: Knit all the way around.

Rounds 4-5: Repeat rounds 2 and 3.

Round 6: Repeat round 1.

Round 7: *P5, K5. Repeat from * to end of round.

Round 8: Knit all the way around.

Rounds 9-10: Repeat rounds 7 and 8.

Round 11: Repeat round 7.

Rounds 12-61: repeat rounds 2-11 5 times.

Rounds 62-64: Knit all the way around. Bind off loosely.

Photo for reference only: http://goo.gl/p1ZeSb

Chunky Afghan May 19

Materials

6 skeins super bulky yarn   Circular knitting needle size 8mm

Directions

Row 1: Work back and forth instead of in rounds. Cast 104 stitches onto the needle.
Row 2: With right side facing, K7. *K2tog, YO, K9. Repeat from * 7 times, K2tog, YO, K7.
Row 3 and all alternate rows: K2, P to last 2 stitches, K2.
Row 4: K6. *(K2tog, YO) twice, K7. Repeat from * 7 times, (K2tog, YO) twice, K6.
Row 6: K5. *(K2tog, YO) 3 times, K5. Repeat from * 7 times, (K2tog, YO) 3 times, K5.
Row 8: K4. *(K2tog, YO) 4 times, K3. Repeat from * 7 times (K2tog YO) 4 times, K4.
Row 10: K3. *(K2tog, YO) 5 times, K1. Repeat from * 7 times, (K2tog, YO) 5 times, K3.
Row 12: Repeat row 8.
Row 14: Repeat row 6.
Row 16: Repeat row 4.
Row 18: Repeat row 3.
Next rows: Repeat rows 2-18 until piece measures 60", ending on 17th row of pattern.
Next rows: Knit 3 rows. Cast off.

Photo for reference only: http://goo.gl/FRZeXT

Barrette May 20

Materials

Chenille yarn   Barette
Knitting needles size 5mm   Glue gun and glue

Directions

Row 1: Cast 12 stitches onto the needle.
Row 2: Knit all the way across.
Next rows: Repeat row 2 until piece measures 6". Bind off.

Finishing

Glue barrette in the center of knitted piece. Fold sides of knitted piece over barrette, and glue in place.

Photo for reference only: http://goo.gl/x09Wzd

KNITTED FLOWER

Materials

Worsted weight yarn   Knitting needles size 2.25mm

Directions

Row 1: Cast 5 stitches onto the needle.
Row 2: *SL1, K3, leave remaining stitch unworked. Turn.
Row 3: P3, leave remaining stitch unworked. Turn.
Row 4: K3, leave remaining stitch unworked. Turn.
Row 5: P3, leave remaining stitch unworked. Turn.
Row 6: K4.
Row 7: P2tog, P1, P2tog.
Row 8: K1, K2tog, p-ass first stitch over leaving 1 stitch on needle. Use this stitch as the first cast-on stitch for the next petal. Work 3-5 petals.

Finishing

Pull thread through final stitch, gather up middle of flower by catching 2 stitches from each petal and pulling them tight. Glue a button or a piece of felt to the center.

Photo for reference only: http://goo.gl/MYhxvU

FLOWER HEADBAND

Materials

1 skein super chunky yarn   Worsted weight yarn
Knitting needles size 10mm   Knitting needles size 2.25mm

Directions

Row 1: With larger needles, cast 35 stitches onto the needle.
Row 2: Knit all the way across.
Row 3: Purl all the way across.
Next rows: Repeat rows 2 and 3 until piece measures 4". Bind off.

Finishing

Fold piece in half and stitch up seam. Make 3-4 flowers from knitted flower pattern and attach them to headband.

Photo for reference only: http://goo.gl/ooBsrH

*F*AST AND *E*ASY *S*HAWL

Materials

5 skeins Red Heart Super Saver worsted weight yarn

Directions

Row 1: With 5 strands of yarn, cast 28 stitches onto your left arm.
Row 2: Knit all the way across.
Row 3: K2tog, K to last 2 stitches, K2tog.
Row 4: Repeat row 3 until there are 4 stitches on the needle.
Next row: K2tog twice. Bind off.

Photo for reference only: http://goo.gl/r7dNna

*S*UPER-*S*IMPLE *S*HRUG

Materials

2 skeins Red Heart Super Saver worsted weight yarn
Circular knitting needle size 9mm

Directions

Row 1: Work back and forth instead of in rounds. Cast 24 stitches onto the needle.
Row 2: With wrong side facing, purl all the way across.
Row 3: Knit all the way across.
Row 4: Purl all the way across.
Row 5: Knit all the way across.
Row 6: Purl all the way across.
Row 7: Knit all the way across, increasing at the first and last stitch.
Next rows: Repeat rows 2-7 until sleeve is desired length.
Next rows: Continue in stockinette stitch for 60 rows. Attach a stitch marker.
Sleeve row 1: With wrong side facing, purl all the way across.
Row 2: Knit all the way across.
Row 3: Purl all the way across.
Row 4: Knit all the way across.
Row 5: Purl all the way across.
Row 6: K2tog, K to last 2 stitches, K2tog.
Next rows: Repeat rows 1-6 8 times.
Next 5 rows: Work in stockinette stitch, ending on purl row. Bind off.

Finishing

Stitch sleeves from edges to markers.

Photo for reference only: http://goo.gl/Enf9eO

Basket Weave Coasters

Materials

Worsted weight yarn

Knitting needles size 4.5mm

Directions

Row 1: Cast 20 stitches onto the needle.
Rows 2-5: K4, P4, K4, P4, K4.
Rows 6-9: P4, K4, P4, K4, P4.
Rows 10-13: Repeat row 2.
Rows 14-17: Repeat row 6.
Rows 18-21: Repeat row 2. Bind off.

Photo for reference only: http://goo.gl/XrnFhc

Foot Cushion

Materials

6 skeins super chunky yarn
Knitting needles size 15mm

Fiberfill stuffing
Yarn needle

Directions

Row 1: Cast 42 stitches onto the needle using 3 strands of yarn.
Row 2: Knit all the way across.
Next rows: Repeat row 2 until piece measures 50". Bind off.

Finishing

Fold piece in half lengthwise, and stitch up side seams. Stuff with fiberfill. Loosely stitch top seam, and pull tight to gather and close opening.

Photo for reference only: http://goo.gl/BiCqiR

Seed Stitch Coasters

Materials

Worsted weight yarn

Knitting needles size 3.5mm

Directions

Row 1: Cast 21 stitches onto the needle.
Row 2: K1. *P1, K1. Repeat from * to end of row.
Next rows: Repeat row 2 until piece is square. Bind off.

Photo for reference only: http://goo.gl/hznnqO

Heart Mini Washcloth

Materials

Cotton worsted weight yarn   Knitting needles size 5mm

Directions

Row 1: Cast 26 stitches onto the needle.
Rows 2-11: SL1, (K5, ssk, K4, KFB) twice, K1.
Row 12: SL1, ssk, K3, ssk, K4, KFB, K5, K2tog, K2, K2tog, KFB, K1.
Row 13: SL1, K4, SSK, K4, KFB, K5, K2tog, K3, KFB, K1.
Row 14: SL1, ssk, K2, ssk, K4, KFB, K5, K2tog, K1, K2tog, KFB, K1.
Row 15: SL1, K3, ssk, K4, KFB, K5, K2tog, K2, KFB, K1.
Row 16: SL1, ssk, K1, K2tog, K4, KFB, K5, K2tog twice, KFB, K1.
Row 17: SL1, ssk twice, K4, KFB, K5, K2tog, K3.
Row 18: SSK twice, K4 KFB, K5, K2tog twice.
Row 19: SSK, K4, KFB, K5, K2tog, K1.
Row 20: SSK, K4, (knit in front, YO, knit in back of same stitch), K3, K2tog twice. Bind off.

Photo for reference only: http://goo.gl/S2LtGn

Knitted Bookmark

Materials

Worsted weight yarn   Knitting needles size 5mm

Directions

Row 1: Cast 10 stitches onto the needle.
Row 2: Knit all the way across.
Row 3: Purl all the way across.
Next rows: Repeat rows 2 and 3 until piece measures 8". Bind off.

Photo for reference only: https://goo.gl/WhSZA3

Toddler Hat

Materials

1 skein Red Heart Super Saver worsted weight yarn
Circular knitting needle size 5mm

Directions

Round 1: Cast 64 stitches onto the needle.
Round 2: *K2, P2. Repeat from * to end of round.

Next rounds: Repeat round 2 until piece measures 2".

Next rounds: Knit all the way around until piece measures 6".

Next round: Place stitch markers every 8 stitches. K to 2 stitches before marker, K2tog. Repeat until end of round.

Next rounds: Repeat last round until there are 4 stitches remaining. Pull yarn through stitches tightly to close opening.

Finishing

Add a pompom to the top of the hat.

PATCHES PILLOW May 31

Materials

1 skein Red Heart Super Saver worsted weight yarn
Scraps of worsted weight yarn in a contrasting color

Knitting needles size 3.75mm
Fiberfill stuffing
Yarn needle

Directions

Make 4 small squares and 1 large square
Small squares
Row 1: Cast 22 stitches onto the needle.
Rows 2-45: Knit all the way across. Bind off.
Large square
Row 1: Cast 55 stitches onto the needle.
Rows 2-111: Knit all the way across. Bind off.

Finishing

Stitch 4 small squares together to form 1 large square. Place on top of large square, and stitch 3 sides. Fill with fiberfill stuffing and stitch shut.

Photo for reference only: http://goo.gl/mUU2C4

How to Start Knitting for Charity

If you are at the point where you are knitting all the time, but you have no one to give your knitted items to, they are going to build up after a while. At this point, you will have two options: stop knitting, which obviously isn't going to be an option; or start giving your knitted items to charity. There are so many organizations that can benefit from this type of donation. For instance, maternity wards in hospitals are always grateful for donations of preemie hats, baby blankets, booties, mittens, etc. If you have considered donating your hand-crafted items to charity, but you don't know how to go about doing it, here are some ideas to get you started.

Homeless Shelters – If you knit mittens, hats, scarves, and socks, your donations will be greatly appreciated at homeless shelters. Blankets are also appreciated, especially during the winter months. If you are not sure where to find shelters in your area, call the local Salvation Army. They will be able to put you in contact with shelters that rely on donations of items from the public. Maybe you even know other knitters who would like to get in on this. The more the better, and those who receive the knitted items really need them.

Women's Shelters – You have a couple of options when it comes to helping women's shelters. Obviously, donations of knitted items for both women and children are always needed. Another option is to become a volunteer. Your skills as a knitter can be put to good use in teaching residents how to knit themselves. Again, if you are unsure of where to find a women's shelter, contact the Salvation Army nearest you to be put in touch with the proper organizations.

Nursing Homes – If you are looking for a way to give back to the community, volunteering at a nursing home is a great way to do it. There are different ways that you can do this. You can simply donate knitted items to various nursing homes. Or, you can donate your time as well, teaching seniors how to knit (or learning a few things you didn't know from seniors who are experienced knitters).

Charity Sales – Many charities sell items at markets, fairs, etc. to raise money. You may want to start donating your knitted items to these charities. Or, you can even have your own sale. For example, you can hold a yard sale. In addition to making extra money by selling old items you no longer want or need, you can sell knitted items and donate the proceeds from the sale of those items to a charity. Another great idea is to sell tickets on a knitted item, such as a blanket or sweater, and donate the funds to a charity.

Youth Organizations – Again, you have the option of donating items, or donating your time. Often, schools offer after-school programs, and they need volunteers to help. You may be interested in teaching kids how to knit. Contact local schools to see if they have these programs and to find out how you can help.

June

Summer is here, and you may not have a lot of time for bigger knitting projects. That's okay, because you can still find time to hone your knitting skills by practicing learning new stitches. This month is another month that is devoted to showing you some of the fancier knitting stitches. You can do up practice pieces in less than an hour, and of course, there will be a project to go along with each new type of stitch you learn.

Knitting Climbing Vine Lace

Materials

Worsted weight yarn
Knitting needles for the project you are working on

Directions

Row 1: Cast 22 stitches onto the needle.
Row 2: Right side facing. K1, P1. *K2tog, yo, K3, yo, ssk, P1. Repeat from * to last stitch, K1.
Row 3: P1. *K1, P7. Repeat from * to last 2 stitches, K1, P1.
Row 4: K1, P1. *K2, yo, SK2P, yo, K2, P1. Repeat from * to last stitch, K1.
Row 5: P1. *K1, P7. Repeat from * to last 2 stitches, K1, P1. Repeat rows 2-5 to create pattern.

Photo for reference only: http://goo.gl/rTRmjb

Climbing Vine Lace Table Runner

Materials

2-3 skeins Red Heart Super Saver yarn   Knitting needles size 4mm

Directions

Row 1: Cast 74 stitches onto the needle.
Rows 2 and 3: Knit all the way across.
Next rows: Follow rows 2-5 of climbing vine lace pattern. Continue in this pattern until piece measures 36".
Next 4 rows: Knit all the way across. Bind off.

Photo for reference only: https://goo.gl/ooib0Y

Knitting a Simple Fair-Isle Pattern

Materials

Worsted weight yarn, 2 colors
Knitting needles for the project you are working on

Directions

Row 1: Cast 27 stitches onto the needle with main color.
Row 2: Purl all the way across.
Row 3: K2. *K1 second color, K3 main color, K1 second color, K3 main color. Repeat from * to last stitch, K1.
Rows 4 and 6: Purl all the way across.
Row 5: Knit all the way across.
Row 6: K2. *K2 main color, K1 second color, K3 main color, K1 second color, K1 main color. Repeat from * to end of row, K1.

Rows 7 and 9: Purl all the way across.
Row 8: Knit all the way across. Repeat rows 2-9 to complete pattern.

Photo for reference only: http://goo.gl/bB3Jce

*F*AIR-ISLE SCARF   June 4

Materials

2 skeins Red Heart Super Saver worsted   Knitting needles size 6mm
weight yarn, different colors

Directions

Row 1: Cast 67 stitches onto the needle.
Rows 2-9: Follow fair-isle pattern until piece measures desired length. Bind off.

*H*OW TO ARM KNIT   June 5

Materials

3 skeins super chunky yarn

Directions

Row 1: Using your arms as needles and three strands of yarn, cast on 10 stitches.
Row 2: Using your arms, knit all the way across.
Row 3: Using your arms, purl all the way across. Repeat knit and purl rows a few times until you get the hang of arm knitting.

Photo for reference only: http://goo.gl/Uzrfdy

*A*RM KNIT BLANKET   June 6

Materials

6 skeins super chunky yarn

Directions

Row 1: Cast on 32 stitches.
Row 2: Knit all the way across.
Row 3: Purl all the way across.
Next rows: Repeat rows 2 and 3 until piece reaches desired length.

Finishing

Add a fringe all the way around the blanket.

Photo for reference only: http://goo.gl/rIZZ3e

KNITTING A 3-STITCH POPCORN BOBBLE

Materials

Worsted weight yarn
Knitting needles for the project you are working on

Directions

Row 1: Cast 20 stitches onto the needle.

Row 2: *K2. Start 3-stitch bobble with right side facing. Insert needle into next stitch, K1, leave stitch on needle. Move yarn to front, P in same stitch. Move yarn to back, K in same stitch. With the wrong side facing, insert needle into all 3 stitches purlwise, P3tog. Repeat from * to last 2 stitches, K2.

Row 3: Purl all the way across.

Row 4: Knit all the way across.

Row 5: Purl all the way across.

Row 6: Repeat row 2.

Next rows: Repeat rows 2-6 until you have a square piece. Bind off.

Photo for reference only: https://goo.gl/7YQ9mL

3-STITCH BOBBLE BABY BLANKET

Materials

2 skeins Red Heart Super Saver worsted weight yarn

Circular knitting needle size 6mm
Crochet hook

Directions

Row 1: Cast 180 stitches onto the needle.

Row 2: Knit all the way around.

Row 3: Purl all the way around.

Row 4: Follow row 2 of 3-stitch bobble instructions.

Row 5: Purl all the way around.

Row 6: Knit all the way around.

Row 7: Purl all the way around.

Next rows: Repeat rows 4-7 until pieces reaches desired size. Bind off.

Finishing

With crochet hook, attach yarn and single crochet all the way around. If you want to create a fancy edge, do another crochet round of shells.

Photo for reference only: http://goo.gl/PwwEgw

KNITTING A 4-STITCH POPCORN BOBBLE   June 9

Materials

Worsted weight yarn
Knitting needles for the project you are working on.

Directions

Cast 20 stitches onto the needle.

Row 2: *K2. Start 3-stitch bobble with right side facing. Insert needle into next stitch, K1, leave stitch on needle. Move yarn to front, P in same stitch. Move yarn to back, K in same stitch. Move yarn to front, P1 in same stitch. With the wrong side facing, insert needle into all 4 stitches purlwise, P4tog. Repeat from * to last 2 stitches, K2.

Row 3: Purl all the way across.

Row 4: Knit all the way across.

Row 5: Purl all the way across.

Row 6: Repeat row 2.

Next rows: Repeat rows 2-6 until you have a square piece. Bind off.

Photo for reference only: http://goo.gl/1X76OP

4-STITCH POPCORN BOBBLE SCARF   June 10

Materials

220 yards super bulky yarn   Knitting needles size 10mm

Directions

Row 1: Cast 50 stitches onto the needle.

Row 2: Knit all the way across.

Row 3: Knit all the way across.

Row 4: K2. *Start 3-stitch bobble with right side facing. Insert needle into next stitch, K1, leave stitch on needle. Move yarn to front, P in same stitch. Move yarn to back, K in same stitch. Move yarn to front, P1 in same stitch. With the wrong side facing, insert needle into all 4 stitches purlwise, P4tog. Repeat from * to last 2 stitches, K2.

Row 5: Knit all the way across.

Row 6: Repeat row 4:

Next rows: Repeat rows 4-5 until pieces reaches desired length.

Last 2 rows: Knit all the way across. Bind off.

Finishing

Add a fringe to either end of the scarf.

Photo for reference only: http://goo.gl/yAhXZl

KNITTING A 5-STITCH POPCORN BOBBLE

Materials

Worsted weight yarn
Knitting needles for the project you are working on.

Directions

Cast 20 stitches onto the needle.

Row 2: *K2. Start 3-stitch bobble with right side facing. Insert needle into next stitch, K1, leave stitch on needle. Move yarn to front, P in same stitch. Move yarn to back, K in same stitch. Move yarn to front, P1 in same stitch. Move yarn to back, K1 in same stitch. With the wrong side facing, insert needle into all 4 stitches purlwise, P4tog, K5. Repeat from * to last 2 stitches, K2.

Row 3: Purl all the way across.

Row 4: Knit all the way across.

Row 5: Purl all the way across.

Row 6: Repeat row 2.

Next rows: Repeat rows 2-6 until you have a square piece. Bind off.

Photo for reference only: https://goo.gl/Vd9W0g

5-STITCH BOBBLE LAP BLANKET

Materials

2-3 skeins Red Heart Super Saver worsted weight yarn
Circular knitting needle size 8mm

Directions

Row 1: Work back and forth instead of in rounds. Cast 250 stitches onto the needle.

Rows 2-5: Knit all the way across.

Row 6: K4. Follow instructions for 5-stitch popcorn bobble, repeat bobble stitch to last 4 stitches, K4.

Next rows: Repeat row 6 until piece is desired size.

Last 4 rows: Knit all the way across. Bind off.

Photo for reference only: http://goo.gl/YR8kWT

KNITTING A KNOT STITCH

Materials

Worsted weight yarn
Knitting needles for the project you are working on

Directions

Row 1: Cast 21 stitches onto the needle.

Row 2: *Insert needle into next 3 stitches, purlwise, P3tog. YO, insert needle into next 3 stitches, purlwise, P3tog. Slip 3 stitches off main needle. Repeat from * to end of row. Repeat this row until you have a square piece. Bind off.

Photo for reference only: http://goo.gl/WsztN3

$\mathcal{K}$NOT STITCH SCARF   June 15

Materials

1 skein Red Heart Super Saver worsted weight yarn
Knitting needles 6mm

Directions

Row 1: Cast 75 stitches onto the needle.
Row 2: Follow the instructions for knitting a knot stitch.
Next rows: Repeat row 2 until piece reaches desired length. Bind off.

Finishing

Add a fringe to either end of the scarf.

Photo for reference only: http://goo.gl/DYnWwg

$\mathcal{K}$NITTING A BIRD'S EYE TRIM   June 16

Materials

Worsted weight yarn
Knitting needles for the project you are working on

Directions

Row 1: Cast 20 stitches onto the needle
Row 2: With right side facing, *K2, YO 3times, K2. Repeat from * to end of row.
Row 3: *K3, P1, K3. Repeat from * to end of row.
Rows 4, 5, and 6: Knit all the way across.
Row 7: *SL first stitch, bind off 3 stitches, K3. Repeat from * to end of row. Bind off.

Photo for reference only: http://goo.gl/N5xGn3

$\mathcal{B}$IRD'S EYE TRIM PLACEMAT   June 17

Materials

1 skein Red Heart Super Saver worsted weight yarn
Knitting needles size 6mm

Directions

Row 1: Cast 68 stitches onto the needle.
Rows 2-7: Follow pattern for knitting a bird's eye trim.
Next rows: Follow a stockinette stitch pattern until piece measures 12".
Last 7 rows: Follow pattern for knitting a bird's eye trim.

Finishing

Pick up stitches along each side of piece (multiple of 4), and follow the bird's eye trim pattern.

Photo for reference only: http://goo.gl/xO9vM1

Knitting Drop Stitch Lace   June 18

Materials

Worsted weight yarn
Knitting needles for the project you are working on

Directions

Row 1: Cast 20 stitches onto the needle
Row 2: Knit all the way across.
Row 3: *K1, K with 3 wraps, (insert needle knitwise, wrap yarn 3 times, pull yarn through stitch to create a stitch with 3 wraps. K1, drop wraps so they unravel.
Row 4: Knit all the way across.
Next rows: Repeat rows 3-4 until piece is a square. Bind off.

Photo for reference only: http://goo.gl/Wsouyz

Drop Stitch Lace Infinity Scarf   June 19

Materials

1 skein Red Heart Super Saver worsted weight yarn
Circular knitting needle size 6.5mm

Directions

Row 1: Cast 200 stitches onto the needle.
Row 2: Knit all the way across.
Next rows: Follow rows 3 and 4 for drop stitch lace instructions until piece measures 12". Bind off.

Photo for reference only: http://goo.gl/rlXqTI

Knitting a Rick Rack Stitch   June 20

Materials

Worsted weight yarn
Knitting needles for the project you are working on

Directions

Row 1: Cast 19 stitches onto the needle.

Row 2: P1. *Sl 1 stitch, insert needle into back of next stitch, K1, knit the stitch you slipped. Slip these 2 stitches onto the left needle, P1. Repeat from * to end of row.

Next rows: Repeat row 2 until piece is square. Bind off.

Photo for reference only: http://goo.gl/WxCvYu

Rick Rack Stitch Table Runner   June 21

Materials

1 skein Red Heart Super Saver worsted weight yarn   Knitting needles size 6mm

Directions

Row 1: Cast 80 stitches onto the needle.

Row 2: Follow the instructions for knitting a rick rack stitch.

Next rows: Repeat row 2 until piece measures 36"-48" (depending on the size of your table). Bind off.

Photo for reference only: http://goo.gl/jD851S

Knitting a Lateral Braid Stitch   June 22

Materials

Worsted weight yarn
Knitting needles for the project you are working on

Directions

Row 1: Cast 20 stitches onto the needle.

Rows 2-5: Knit in stockinette stitch pattern.

Row 6: *Sk first stitch, knit into back loop of second stitch. Knit into front of first stitch, drop both stitches. Slip first stitch from right needle back onto left needle. Repeat from * to last stitch, K, pass second stitch on right needle over.

Rows 7-10: Repeat row 2.

Row 11: Repeat row 6. Repeat pattern until piece is square. Bind off.

Photo for reference only: https://goo.gl/F7xELn

Lateral Braid Stitch Leg Warmers   June 23

Materials

1 skein Red Heart Super Saver worsted weight yarn
3-4 double pointed knitting needles size 6mm and 7mm

Directions

Round 1: Cast 68 stitches onto the needles evenly.

Next rounds: Knit in a rib stitch pattern until piece measures 3".

Next 5 rounds: Knit all the way around.

Next round: Repeat row 6 of lateral braid stitch pattern.

Next rounds: Repeat last 6 rounds until piece measures 15".

Next rounds: Work in rib stitch pattern until piece measures 18". Bind off.

Photo for reference only: https://goo.gl/JG82ca

KNITTING A QUILTED CHECKERED PATTERN   June 24

Materials

Worsted weight yarn, 2 colors
Knitting needles for the project you are working on

Directions

Row 1: Cast 23 stitches onto the needle with MC.

Row 2: Knit all the way across.

Row 3: With wrong side facing, P4. *Sl3, yarn in back, P3. Repeat from * to last stitch, P1.

Row 4: With color B, K5. *SL1 with yarn in front, K5. Repeat from * to end of row.

Row 5: With color A, K5. *K1 under loose strand, K5. Repeat from * to end of row.

Row 6: With color A, P1. *SL3 with yarn in back, P3. Repeat from * to last 4 stitches, SL 3 with yarn in back, P1.

Row 7: With color B, K2. *SL1 with yarn in front, K5. Repeat from * to last 3 stitches, SL1 with yarn in front, K2.

Row 8: With color B, P2. *SL1 with yarn in back, P5. Repeat from * to last 3 stitches, SL1 with yarn in back, P2.

Row 9: With color A, K2. *K1 under loose strand, K5. Repeat from * to last 3 stitches, K1 under loose strand, K2. Repeat rows 2-9 until piece is square. Bind off.

Photo for reference only: http://goo.gl/pZIWnh

QUILTED CHECKERED PATTERN COUCH BLANKET   June 25

Materials

2 skeins each of 2 colors Red Heart Super Saver worsted weight yarn
Circular knitting needle size 6.5mm

Directions

Row 1: Work back and forth and not in the round. Cast 203 stitches onto the needle.

Row 2: Knit all the way across.

Row 3: With wrong side facing, P4. *Sl3, yarn in back, P3. Repeat from * to last stitch, P1.

Row 4: With color B, K5. *SL1 with yarn in front, K5. Repeat from * to end of row.

Row 5: With color A, K5. *K1 under loose strand, K5. Repeat from * to end of row.

Row 6: With color A, P1. *SL3 with yarn in back, P3. Repeat from * to last 4 stitches, SL 3 with yarn in back, P1.

Row 7: With color B, K2. *SL1 with yarn in front, K5. Repeat from * to last 3 stitches, SL1 with yarn in front, K2.

Row 8: With color B, P2. *SL1 with yarn in back, P5. Repeat from * to last 3 stitches, SL1 with yarn in back, P2.

Row 9: With color A, K2. *K1 under loose strand, K5. Repeat from * to last 3 stitches, K1 under loose strand, K2. Repeat rows 2-9 until piece reaches desired size. Bind off.

Finishing

Add a fringe all the way around the blanket.

Photo for reference only: http://goo.gl/SY4c1m

Knitting a Reversible Grand Eyelet Stitch   June 27

Materials

Worsted weight yarn
Knitting needles for the pattern you are working on

Directions

Row 1: Cast 20 stitches onto the needle.

Row 2: P2. *YO, P4tog. Repeat from * to last 2 stitches, P2.

Row 3: K2. *K1, (K1, P1, K1) into YO. Repeat from * to last 2 stitches, K2.

Row 4: Knit all the way across.

Next rows: Repeat rows 2-4 until piece is square. Bind off.

Photo for reference only: http://goo.gl/Ej8qHS

Reversible Grand Eyelet Wrap   June 28

Materials

2 skeins Red Heart Super Saver worsted weight yarn
Knitting needles size 7mm

Directions

Row 1: Cast 86 stitches onto the needle.

Rows 2-7: Knit all the way across.

Row 8: Knit 6. *YO, P4tog. Repeat from * to last 6 stitches, K6.

Row 9: Knit 6. *K1, (K1, P1, K1) into YO. Repeat from * to last 6 stitches, K6.

Row 10: Knit all the way across.

Next rows: Repeat rows 8-10 until piece reaches desired length. Bind off.

Photo for reference only: http://goo.gl/gnWeJN

KNITTING VALENTINE LACE

Materials

Worsted weight yarn
Knitting needles for the project you are working on

Directions

Row 1: Cast 25 stitches onto the needle.
Row 2: K1. *YO, K2tog, K3, YO, K1, YO, K3, SL1, K1, PSSO, YO, K1. Repeat from * to end of row.
Row 3 and all uneven rows: Purl all the way across.
Row 4: K2. *YO, K4tog, YO, K3. Repeat to last 2 stitches, K2.
Row 6: K1. *K1, K2tog, YO, K5, YO, SL1, K1, PSSO, K2. Repeat from * to end of row.
Row 8: K2tog, YO, K9, YO. *SL1, K2tog, PSSO, YO, K9, YO. Repeat from * to last 2 stitches, SL1, K1, PSSO.
Row 9: Purl all the way across.
Next rows: Repeat rows 2-9 until piece is square. Bind off.

Photo for reference only: http://goo.gl/YYV5C5

VALENTINE LACE SCARF

Materials

1 skein Red Heart Super Saver worsted weight yarn
Knitting needles size 6mm

Directions

Row 1: Cast 73 stitches onto the needle.
Rows 2-9: Follow pattern rows 2-9 for Valentine lace.
Next rows: Repeat rows 2-9 until piece reaches desired length. Bind off.

Finishing

Add a fringe to either end of the scarf.

Photo for reference only: http://goo.gl/bS6GVj

WHERE TO SELL YOUR KNITTED ITEMS

It may be that you have a lot of knitted items, and nothing to do with them. Have you considered selling them? There are several ways that you can make money with your knitting. Sure, you knit because you love knitting. But, if there is a chance that you can pocket some extra cash, why not give it a try? Here are some of the best ways to sell hand-made knitted items.

Online – There are many ways that you can use the Internet to your advantage and make money selling your knitted items. If you don't want to set up your own website, there are other options available. Etsy is a popular site for selling hand-crafted items. Another option is eBay, and other similar auction sites. You will have to do your research to find the best online options for you.

Local Stores – While it is unlikely that you will be able to sell your items at larger chain stores, there are probably all kinds of local retailers who would love to sell hand-crafted items. This is especially true during peak tourist seasons, when people are looking for items that are made by local crafters. Start calling on local retailers to see if they would be interested in selling your work on consignment.

Consignment Stores – Another local retail option is the consignment store. It is usually pretty easy to get your work into these stores, because there is no risk to the store owners. They display your items, and if the items sell, they take a percentage of the sale. Generally, you get 60% and the consignment store gets 40%, but the numbers can vary from store to store, and from city to city.

Markets – Attending markets is a great way to sell your knitted items, and there are usually a variety of markets, festivals, and craft fairs that you can take part in. Most of the time, you can rent a space for $20 or less per day. Depending on the type of market and the location, you may be required to bring your own table. If it is an outdoor market, you may also want to consider having a canopy of some sort, to protect you and your knitted items from the sun.

July

It's time to celebrate, and nothing says Fourth of July celebrations like a good, old-fashioned barbecue. What is going to set your barbecue apart from the rest is the decorations, because many of them will be items that you have knitted yourself. This month, you will find patterns for fun placemats, beer can cozies, coasters, and a whole lot more. So, find yourself a comfy spot outside, grab your knitting stuff, and get ready to celebrate.

Summer Scarf July 1

Materials

Light weight or sport weight yarn   Circular knitting needle size 6mm

Directions

Row 1: Work back and forth, and not in rounds. Cast 240 stitches onto the needle.
Row 2: Knit all the way across.
Next rows: Repeat row 2 until piece measures 8-10" wide. Bind off.

Finishing

Add a fringe to either end of the scarf.

Photo for reference only: http://goo.gl/2eTJs0

Patriotic Placemat July 2

Materials

Red, white, and blue worsted weight yarn   Knitting needles size 6.5mm

Directions

Row 1: Cast 70 onto the needle with white yarn.
Row 2: Knit all the way across.
Rows 3-5: Repeat row 2.
Row 5: K4. Switch to red yarn, and knit to last 4 stitches. K4 with white yarn.
Rows 6-8: Repeat row 5.
Rows 9-12: Repeat row 2 with white yarn.
Row 13: K4 with white yarn. Switch to blue yarn, and knit to last 4 stitches. K4 with white yarn.
Rows 14-16: Repeat row 9.
Rows 17-20: Repeat row 2 with white yarn. Continue working in a white, red, white, blue pattern until piece reaches desired size. Bind off.

Photo for reference only: https://goo.gl/HP8J6V

Patriotic Coasters July 3

Materials

Red, white, and blue worsted weight yarn   Knitting needles size 6.5mm

Directions

Row 1: Cast 20 stitches onto the needle with red yarn.
Row 2: Knit all the way across.
Row 3: Repeat row 2.

Row 4: Switch to white yarn, and repeat row 2.

Row 5: Repeat row 2.

Row 6: Switch back to red yarn, and repeat row 2.

Row 7: Repeat row 2.

Row 8: Repeat row 4.

Row 9: Repeat row 5.

Row 10: Switch to blue yarn, K7. Switch back to white yarn and knit the rest of the way across.

Row 11: K7 with blue yarn, knit with white yarn the rest of the way across.

Row 12: K7 with blue yarn, knit with red yarn the rest of the way across.

Row 13: Repeat row 12.

Row 14: Repeat row 11.

Row 15: Repeat row 11.

Row 16: Repeat row 12.

Row 17: Repeat row 12. Bind off.

Photo for reference only: https://goo.gl/JQ8odK

$\mathcal{P}$ATRIOTIC SUMMER SCARF   July 4

Materials

Red, white, and blue Red Heart Super Saver worsted weight yarn
Circular knitting needle size 6mm
Yarn needle

Directions

Row 1: Work back and forth and not in rounds. Cast 160 stitches onto the needle with white yarn.

Row 2: Knit all the way across.

Rows 3-6: Repeat row 2.

Rows 7-11: Switch to red yarn and repeat row 2.

Rows 12-16: Switch to white yarn and repeat row 2.

Rows 17-21: Switch to blue yarn and repeat row 2.

Rows 22-26: Switch to white yarn and repeat row 2.

Rows 27-31: Switch to red yarn and repeat row 2.

Rows 32-36: Switch to white yarn and repeat row 2. Bind off.

Finishing

Add a red, white, and blue fringe to either end of the scarf. With yarn needle, embroider white stars along the red and blue sections.

Photo for reference only: http://goo.gl/ysMlqx

Cute Tank Top

Materials

300 yards cotton yarn
Knitting needles size 5.5mm

Yarn needle

Directions

Pattern written in small size. Larger sizes are in brackets.

Back

Row 1: Cast 60 (64, 68, 72) stitches onto the needle.
Row 2: Knit all the way across.
Row 3: Purl all the way across.
Next rows: Repeat rows 2 and 3 until piece measures 14.5" (15", 15.5", 16").
First armhole row: Bind off first 3 stitches. Continue in stockinette stitch.
Next row: Repeat last row.
Next 2 rows: Bind off first 2 stitches. Continue in stockinette stitch.
Next row: Decrease 1 stitch, continue in stockinette stitch to last stitch, decrease.
Next row: Continue in stockinette stitch.
Next rows: Repeat last 2 rows until there are 44 (48, 52, 56) stitches remaining. Continue working in stockinette stitch until piece measures 21" (22", 23", 24"). Bind off loosely.

Front

Work pattern the same as for the back, until piece measures 16" (17", 18", 19"), ending on a wrong side row. Begin shaping the neck.
Neck row 1: Working in stockinette stitch, do 12 (14, 16, 18) stitches, bind off 20 stitches, continue knitting to end of row.
Next rows: Continue working in stockinette stitch on each side until piece measures 21" (22", 23", 24"), ending on a wrong side row. Bind off loosely.

Finishing

Stitch up the side seams. Using the crochet hook, single crochet all around the neck hole and arm holes to reinforce them and give a more finished look.

Photo for reference only: http://goo.gl/bXG1QR

Beach Bag

Materials

1 skein Red Heart Super Saver worsted weight yarn
Knitting needles size 4.5mm
Yarn needle
Crochet hook

Directions

Make 2

Row 1: Cast 50 stitches onto the needle.
Rows 2-5: Knit all the way across.
Row 6: Knit all the way across.
Row 7: K5. *YO, K2tog. Repeat from * to last 5 stitches, K5.
Next rows: Repeat rows 6 and 7 until piece measures 14". Bind off.

Finishing

Place both pieces together, and stitch bottom and side seams. With crochet hook, make a chain that is approximately 36", using 2-3 strands of yarn. Weave chain through the top section of the bag to create a drawstring, and tie the ends of the chain together to create a shoulder strap.

Photo for reference only: http://goo.gl/9rjHhi

BEACH BLANKET BAG   July 7

Materials

2-3 skeins Red Heart Super Saver worsted weight yarn
Knitting needles size 8mm
Circular knitting needle size 8mm
Yarn needle

Directions

Main Section

Row 1: Work back and forth, not in rounds. Cast 100 stitches onto the circular needle.
Row 2: Knit all the way across
Row 3: Purl all the way across.
Next rows: Continue working in stockinette stitch until piece measures 104". Bind off.

Sides and strap

Row 1: Cast 20 stitches onto the needle.
Row 2: Knit all the way across.
Row 3: Purl all the way across.
Next rows: Continue working in stockinette stitch until piece measures 56". Bind off.

Finishing

Lay main piece flat, and mark at 16". Stitch side/strap piece along one side to the side of the blanket section. Fold blanket section, and stitch the bottom of the side/strap piece. Fold blanket the rest of the way and stitch up the other side. Repeat on the opposite side of the bag. Roll up the blanket and stuff it into the bag section.

Photo for reference only: https://goo.gl/2ETF7q

EACH BLANKET AND PILLOW

July 8

Materials

2-3 skeins Red Heart Super Saver worsted
weight yarn
Circular knitting needle size 7mm

Yarn needle
Fiberfill stuffing

Directions

Row 1: Work back and forth, not in rounds. Cast 100 stitches onto the circular needle.
Row 2: Knit all the way across
Row 3: Purl all the way across.
Next rows: Continue working in stockinette stitch until piece measures 104". Bind off.

Finishing

Mark piece at 16". Fold at this mark, and stitch along the sides. Stuff this section, and then stitch along the bottom of the section.

Photo for reference only: http://goo.gl/iKpDQS

ANKLE BRACELET

July 9

Materials

Cotton finger weight yarn
Knitting needle size 4.5mm

Pony beads
Crochet hook

Directions

Row 1: Cast on enough stitches (multiple of 5 stitches) to give you a length of 10".
Row 2: Knit all the way across.
Row 3: *K5, add a bead. Repeat from * to last 5 stitches, K5.
Row 4: Repeat row 2. Bind off.

Finishing

Insert crochet hook at either end, and create a chain measuring 3-4". This will be for tying the bracelet around the wrist.

Photo for reference only: https://goo.gl/I0qzcV

EER CAN COZY

July 10

Materials

Worsted weight yarn
4 double pointed knitted needles size
4mm

Directions

Round 1: Cast 36 stitches onto the needles.
Round 2: Knit all the way around.
Next rounds: Repeat round 2 until piece measures 4". Bind off.

Photo for reference only: http://goo.gl/gYIgYa

Baby Bib   July 11

Materials

Worsted weight yarn   Button
Knitting needles size 4.5mm   Needle and thread

Directions

Row 1: Cast 34 stitches onto the needle.
Row 2: Knit all the way across.
Next rows: Repeat row 2 until piece measures 8".
Next row: K10, cast off 14 stitches, K10.
Next rows (first strap): Knit until strap measures 5".
Next row: K2tog, K6, K2tog. Bind off.
Next rows (second strap): Repeat strap rows.

Finishing

Sew a button onto one of the straps, and use a crochet hook or knitting needle to open a space on the other strap to act as a buttonhole.

Photo for reference only: http://goo.gl/Fp2TYw

Box Stitch Baby Blanket   July 12

Materials

5 ounces baby yarn   Knitting needles size 6mm

Directions

Row 1: Cast 70 stitches onto the needle.
Rows 2-7: Knit all the way across.
Next rows: Work in box stitch pattern until piece measures 13".
Next 6 rows: Knit all the way across. Bind off.

Photo for reference only: http://goo.gl/GwoUlp

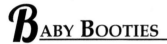 BABY BOOTIES

Materials

Worsted weight yarn   Yarn needle
Knitting needles size 4mm

Directions

Make 2
Row 1: Cast 31 stitches onto needle.
Rows 2-9: Knit all the way across.
Row 10: K12, K2tog, K3, K2tog, K12.
Row 11: K11, K2tog, K3, K2tog, K11.
Row 12: K10, K2tog, K3, K2tog, K10.
Row 13: K9, K2tog, K3, K2tog, K9.
Row 14: K8, K2tog, K3, K2tog, K8.
Row 15: K7, K2tog, K3, K2tog, K7.
Next 12 rows: Knit all the way across. Bind off loosely.

Finishing

Fold piece in half and stitch along front, bottom, and back.

Photo for reference only: http://goo.gl/7mOabB

PREEMIE RIBBED HAT

Materials

Lightweight yarn   Yarn needle
Knitting needles size 4mm

Directions

Row 1: Cast 46 stitches onto the needle.
Row 2: S1, K to end of row.
Rows 3-5: Repeat row 2.
Row 6: S1, K to end of row.
Row 7: S1, P to last stitch, K1.
Row 8: S1, K to end of row.
Row 9: S1, K to end of row.
Rows 10-13: Repeat row 9.
Row 14: *K3, K2tog. Repeat from * to last stitch, K1.
Row 15: S1, P to last stitch, K1.
Row 16: S1, K to end of row.
Row 17: S1, K to end of row.
Row 18: *K2, K2tog. Repeat from * to last stitch, K1.

Row 19: S1, P to last stitch, K1.
Row 20: *K1, K2tog. Repeat from * to last stitch, K1.
Row 21: S1. *K2tog. Repeat from * to last stitch, K1.
Row 22: S1, P to last stitch, K1. Thread yarn through remaining stitches and pull tightly.

Finishing

Stitch along seam to close hat.

Photo for reference only: http://goo.gl/DxWVqU

Easy Shoulder Bag   July 15

Materials

1 skein worsted weight yarn   Yarn needle
Knitting needles size 6mm   Crochet hook

Directions

Row 1: Cast 40 stitches onto the needle.
Row 2: Knit all the way across.
Row 3: Purl all the way across.
Next rows: Work in stockinette stitch pattern until piece measures 22". Bind off.

Finishing

With crochet hook and 3 strands of yarn, crochet a chain measuring 30". Fold knitted piece in half, and stitch the side seams. Attach chain at either side of the bag.

Photo for reference only: https://goo.gl/Ft1Hra

Knitted Bikini Top   July 16

Materials

100 grams soft cotton yarn
4 double pointed knitting needles size 4mm

Directions

Pattern written in small size. Larger sizes are in brackets.
Row 1: Cast 76 (84, 92) stitches evenly on the 4 needles.
Rows 2-13: Knit all the way across.
Next rows: Work the first 38 (42, 46) stitches, place remaining stitches on a stitch holder. Continue working in garter stitch for 12 rows.
Next row: Knit all the way across.
Next rows: With right side facing, increase to 42 (46, 50) stitches. Insert a stitch marker after 21 (23, 25) stitches. Decrease 2 stitches on every other row and 4th row alternately. Continue decreasing until there are 6 stitches on the row. Work remaining 6 stitches for strap.

Strap rows: *4 rows garter stitch, 4 rows stocking stitch. Repeat from * until piece measures 12" or desired length. Bind off.

Other side: Slip stitches off stitch holder and follow pattern the same as for the first side.

Back strap: Pick up 8 stitches in the garter stitches at the side of the bottom of the bikini top. *4 rows garter stitch, 4 rows stockinette stitch. Repeat from * and cast off when strap measures 10". Repeat on other side.

Photo for reference only: http://goo.gl/8i2ntf

$\mathcal{B}$IKINI SHORTS July 17

Materials

250-300 grams soft cotton yarn

Circular knitting needles size 3.5 mm and 4mm

Directions

Pattern written in size small. Larger sizes are in brackets.

Round 1: Cast 140 (156, 168, 184, 196, 212) stitches onto the smaller needle. Use a stitch marker to keep track of rounds.

Round 2: *K2, P2. Repeat from * to end of round, placing a stitch marker after 70 (78, 84, 92, 98, 106) stitches.

Next rounds: Repeat round 2 until piece measures 6". Switch to larger needle.

Next rounds: Work in stockinette stitch, decreasing 0 (1, 0, 1, 0, 1) stitches on both sides of stitch marker of each row so there are 140 (154, 168, 182, 196, 210) stitches. Now, increase 1 stitch on each side of stitch marker every 1" (1, 1, 1, 1.25, 1.25) 8 times, until there are 172 (186, 200, 214, 228, 242) stitches on the needle. When piece measures 13" (13, 13.5, 14, 14.5, 15), cast off first 6 (6, 7, 7, 8, 8) stitches in round, slip next 75 (81, 87, 93, 99, 105) stitches onto a stitch holder. Cast off last 5 (6, 6, 7, 7, 8) stitches. Work 3.5" (4, 4.25, 4.5, 5, 5.25) in stockinette stitch for guesset. Cast off and stitch gusset to the 11 (12, 13, 14, 15, 16) stitches that were cast off mid-back.

Leg rounds: Slip the stitches from the holder back onto the needle. Pick up 17 (19, 21, 23, 25, 27) stitches on side of gusset for a total of 92 (100, 108, 116, 124, 132) stitches. Work in stockinette stitch until leg section measures 1.75" (1.75, 2, 2, 2.25, 2.25) inches. Repeat on other leg and bind off.

Photo for reference only: http://goo.gl/eIxokV

$\mathcal{B}$IKINI SKIRT July 18

Materials

440-650 grams soft cotton yarn
Circular knitting needle sizes 3.5mm and 4mm

Directions

Pattern written in size small. Larger sizes are in brackets.

Round 1: Cast 140 (160, 180, 200, 200) stitches onto the smaller needle.

Rounds 2-5: Work garter stitch all the way around.

Round 6: *K2tog, 1YO. Repeat from * to end of round (eyelet round).

Round 7: Change to larger needle, work in stockinette stitch, inserting stitch markers every 14 (16, 18, 20, 22) stitches.

Next rounds: Working in stockinette stitch, increase 1 stitch before each stitch marker. Repeat every 10th round, 4 times, for a total of 180 (200, 220, 240, 260) stitches.

Next rounds: When piece measures 12.5" (13 ½, 14 ¼, 15, 15 ¾), work in garter stitch next 8 rows.

Next round: *K1, 1YO. Repeat from * to end of round.

Next 8 rounds: Knit all the way around. Bind off.

Finishing

Crochet a chain long enough to wrap around your waist and tie in a bow. Thread through the eyelet row at the top of the bikini skirt.

Photo for reference only: http://goo.gl/KDzTac

Cable Stitch Wrist Cuff   July 19

Materials

Worsted weight yarn
Knitting needles size 4.5mm

Yarn needle

Directions

Row 1: Cast 14 stitches onto the needle.

Rows 2, 4, 6, and 8: K3, P8, K3.

Row 3: P3, slip 2 stitches onto cable needle and hold in back, K2, K stitches from cable needle, slip 2 stitches onto cable needle and hold in front, K2, K stitches from cable needle, P3.

Rows 5, 7, and 9: P3, K8, P3. Bind off.

Finishing

Fold piece in half and stitch along seam.

Photo for reference only: http://goo.gl/GyP0xz

Book Cozy   July 20

Materials

Bulky weight yarn
Knitting needles size 9mm

Yarn needle

Directions

Row 1: Cast 15 stitches onto the needle.

Next rows: Work in stockinette stitch until piece measures 19". Bind off.

Finishing

Fold piece in half lengthwise and stitch seam.

Photo for reference only: http://goo.gl/ZZ1dQ5

REVERSIBLE SCARF

Materials

2 skeins chunky yarn   Knitting needles size 8mm

Directions

Row 1: Cast 26 stitches onto the needle.
Row 2: K3. *Slip 1 stitch with yarn in front, K3. Repeat from * to end of row.
Row 3: K1. *Slip 1 stitch with yarn in front, K3. Repeat from * to last 2 stitches, slip 1, K1.
Next rows: Repeat rows 2 and 3 until piece reaches desired length. Bind off.

Finishing

Add a fringe to each end of the scarf.

Photo for reference only: http://goo.gl/n5lfFA

TEABAG CASE

Materials

Worsted weight yarn   Button
Knitting needles size 6mm   Needle and thread
Yarn needle

Directions

Row 1: Cast 16 stitches onto the needle.
Row 2: Knit all the way across.
Row 3: K4, P8, K4.
Row 4: Knit all the way across.
Row 5: Repeat row 3.
Row 6: Repeat row 4.
Next rows: Repeat rows 3 and 4 until piece measures 6".
Next rows: Decrease 1 stitch at the beginning and end of each row until there are 2 stitches left. Bind off.

Finishing

Mark beginning of flap, and fold the rest in half. Stitch along the sides. Sew a button to the front.

Photo for reference only: http://goo.gl/nnDkWt

PLEATED SKIRT

Materials

400 grams cotton, 4-ply yarn
Circular knitting needles size 3.5mm and 3.75mm

Directions

Round 1: Cast 140 stitches onto the smaller needle.

Round 2: *K1, P1. Repeat from * to end of round.

Next rounds: Repeat round 2 until piece measures 5".

Next round: *K1, YO1, P1, YO1. Repeat from * to end of round. 280 stitches on needle.

Next rounds: *K2, P2. Repeat from * to end of round. Repeat this round until section measures 6".

Next round: *K2, YO1, P2, YO1. Repeat from * to end of round. 420 stitches on needle.

Next rounds: *K3, P3. Repeat from * to end of round. Repeat this round until section measures 8".

Next round: *K3, YO1, P3, YO1. Repeat from * to end of round. 560 stitches on needle.

Next rounds: *K4, P4. Repeat from * to end of round. Repeat this round until section measures 10". Bind off.

Waist band: Take out chain of waist yarn from cast on, pick up loops so there are 140 stitches on the needle. Knit all the way around for 1". Pearl 1 round (folding row), and then knit for another inch. Bind off. Place elastic on this section, fold back waistband, and stitch in place with the elastic.

Photo for reference only: http://goo.gl/QS7jRt

SOOTHING EYE BAG

Materials

Worsted weight yarn
Knitting needles size 6mm
Yarn needle

Muslin bag (4X5")
Flax seeds

Directions

Row 1: Cast 25 stitches onto the needle.

Next rows: Work in stockinette stitch until piece measures 5". Bind off.

Finishing

Fill muslin bag with flax seeds and sew shut. Fold knitted piece in half, and stitch along the sides. Place muslin bag inside, and stitch along the top.

Photo for reference only: http://goo.gl/AR5QQB

INFANT SLEEPING BAG

Materials

1 skein Red Heart Super Saver worsted weight yarn

Circular knitting needle size 5mm

Directions

Special abbreviations: C4F – Place first 2 stitches on a cable needle, hold them to the front, knit the next 2 stitches, knit stitches on cable needle. C4B – Same as C4F, only yarn is held in back.

Round 1: Cast 86 stitches onto the needle.
Rounds 2-17: Work in stockinette stitch.
Round 18: P1. *P2, K8, P2. Repeat from * to end of round.
Round 19: P1. *P2, C4F, C4B, P2. Repeat from * to end of round.
Rounds 20-22: P1. *P2, K8, P2. Repeat from * to end of round.
Round 22: Repeat round 19.
Rounds 23-30: Repeat round 18.
Round 31: Repeat round 19.
Round 32: P1. *P4, K4, P4. Repeat from * to end of round.
Round 33: Knit all the way around.
Round 34: *K17, place stitch marker. Repeat from * to end of round.
Round 35: *K2tog, SM, SSK, K to 2 stitches before marker. Repeat from * to end of round.
Round 36: Knit all the way around.
Next rounds: Repeat rounds 35 and 36 until there are 3 stitches between each stitch marker. Bind off.

Photo for reference only: http://goo.gl/yXoeUe

SUMMER SHAWL

Materials

2 skeins Red Heart Super Saver worsted weight yarn

Circular knitting needle size 6mm
Yarn needle

Directions

Row 1: Work back and forth and not in rounds. Cast 5 stitches onto the needle.
Row 2: K1, YO, K1, YO, place stitch marker, K1, YO, K1, YO.
Row 3: Knit all the way across.
Row 4: Purl all the way across.
Rows 5-10: Repeat rows 3 and 4.
Row 11: Knit all the way across.
Row 12, begin garter stitch pattern: K1, YO. Knit to stitch marker, YO, SM, K1, SM, YO. K to last stitch, YO, K1.
Row 13: Knit all the way across.

Next rows: Repeat rows 12 and 13 3 times.

Next rows: Repeat garter pattern 5 times. Switch to stockinette stitch pattern.

Next row, begin stockinette pattern: K1, YO, K to marker, YO, SM, K1, SM, YO, K to stitch before last, YO, K1.

Next row: Purl all the way across.

Next rows: Repeat last 2 rows 3 times.

Next rows, begin lace row: K1, YO, K1. *YO, K2tog. Repeat from * to marker, YO, SM, K1, SM. **YO, K2tog. Repeat from ** until there are 2 stitches left, YO, K1, YO, K1.

Next row: Purl all the way across.

Next rows: Repeat garter pattern 3 times. Bind off.

Photo for reference only: http://goo.gl/bsKqDU

SIMPLE RIBBED BABY BLANKET   July 27

Materials

2 skeins Red Heart Super Saver worsted weight yarn
Circular knitting needle size 6.5mm

Directions

Row 1: Cast 150 stitches onto the needle.

Row 2: *K3, P3. Repeat from * to end of row.

Next rows: Repeat row 2 until pieces reaches desired size. Cast off.

Photo for reference only: http://goo.gl/SeROvQ

HANKY   July 28

Materials

Worsted weight yarn   Knitting needles size 6mm

Directions

Row 1: Cast 30 stitches onto the needle.

Row 2: Knit all the way across.

Next rows: Repeat row 2 until piece is square. Bind off.

Photo for reference only: http://goo.gl/8y1x0Q

KNITTED KERCHIEF   July 29

Materials

Worsted weight yarn   Crochet hook
Knitting needles size 5mm

Directions

Row 1: Cast 3 stitches onto the needle.
Row 2: Knit all the way across.
Row 3: K1, M1, K1, M1, K1.
Row 4: Knit all the way across.
Row 5: K1, M1, K to last stitch, M1, K1.
Next rows: Repeat rows 4 and 5 until piece measures 9 from point to upper row. Bind off.

Finishing

Insert crochet hook at one of the long corners, and crochet a chain measuring 12". Repeat on other side.

Photo for reference only: http://goo.gl/DbHxm8

ILLOW July 30

Materials

1 skein Red Heart Super Saver worsted weight yarn
Knitting needles size 6.5mm

Crochet hook
Pillow form

Directions

Make 2
Row 1: Cast on enough stitches to make piece long enough to fit across width of the pillow form, with an inch to spare on either side.
Next rows: Work in stockinette stitch until piece is 2 inches longer than the length of the pillow form. Cast off.

Finishing

Place pieces together, wrong sides facing. Single crochet along 3 sides. Insert the pillow form, and single crochet to close.

Photo for reference only: http://goo.gl/VWZJs4

BASKET WEAVE BABY BLANKET July 31

Materials

2-3 skeins Red Heart Super Saver worsted weight yarn
Circular knitting needle size 5mm

Directions

Row 1: Work back and forth and not in rounds. Cast 180 stitches onto needle.
Rows 2-7: 6 seed stitches. *K6, P6. Repeat from * to last 6 stitches, 6 seed stitches.
Rows 8-13: 6 seed stitches. *P6, K6. Repeat from * to last 6 stitches, 6 seed stitches.
Next rows: Repeat rows 2-13 22 times. Bind off.

Photo for reference only: http://goo.gl/4ENqGw

How to Price Your Hand-Made Knitted Items for Sale

When you are selling your hand-made knitted items, it can be difficult to figure out how much to sell them for. After all, you don't want to charge so much that no one buys them, but not so little that it isn't worth your time and effort. There are so many things to consider when you are pricing your knitted items. For instance, are there others who are also selling knitted items, and if so, what are they charging? Here are some things you need to consider when setting prices for your knitted items.

Your Market

The first thing you need to consider is your market, and what they are looking for. If you have something unique, you automatically have an edge over your competition (until they start copying the idea and then you need to step up your game and create something new). You also need to look at how well other crafters do by selling their work in your area. It may be that you will have to go further to make sales, and that may or may not be worth it. You should also look into local boutiques and shops that will be willing to help you sell your items.

It is a good idea to start checking out craft fairs, craft stores, etc. to see what people are buying. Don't actually get a table yet. Simply walk around and see what others are selling, and what the customers are most interested in. Be sure to take note of what other knitters are pricing their items at. If they are selling at low prices, you will have to price your items at this same level in order to make any sales. Or, you could go to other areas where crafters are able to charge more.

Your Cost

Another thing that you need to consider when pricing your knitted items is the cost of the materials that you are using. Remember, just because you are using expensive materials, it doesn't necessarily mean that you will be able to charge a higher price. It is best, at least in the beginning, to use cheaper yarn. This doesn't mean that you will be skimping on quality. For instance, Red Heart yarn is inexpensive, and very high quality. You can make an afghan for about $20-$25, and charge $50-$75 or more, depending on the intricacy of the stitches. A good rule of thumb to go by is to price items at about three times higher than what it cost to make them.

Your Time

You also need to take into consideration the amount of time it took to complete a project when setting a price. Depending on the piece, it could end up that you are making far less than minimum wage. But, remember, you are doing this first and foremost because you love knitting. Any money you make is just gravy on the fries. It is a good idea to stick with smaller pieces that you can make in a few hours, such as hats, mittens, scarves, placemats, coasters, ornaments, etc. The more you can make in a short amount of time, the more money you are going to make.

August

There is still a month or more of warm, summer weather, so you still have plenty of time to sit outside with your knitting. The kids will be heading back to school in a few weeks, so this is a perfect time to start making fun back-to-school items, including book straps and totes, cute headbands, adorable hair bows, and a whole lot more. These are ideal summer afternoon projects that you can make in a few hours while you are on the deck or at the beach.

Lunch Bag

Materials

1 skein Red Heart Super Saver worsted weight yarn

Knitting needles size 6mm
Yarn needle

Directions

Row 1: Cast 90 stitches onto the needle.
Row 2: Knit all the way across.
Row 3: *K5, P5. Repeat from * to end of row.
Rows 4-9: Repeat row 3.
Row 10: Knit all the way across.
Row 11: *P5, K5. Repeat from * to end of row.
Rows 12-17: Repeat rows 2-17 3 times.
Rows 18-28: Knit all the way across.
Row 29: K18, BO14, K26, BO14, K8.
Row 30: K8, CO14, K26, CO14, K18.
Rows 31-37: Knit all the way across. Bind off.

Finishing

Fold piece in half and stitch bottom and side seam.

Photo for reference only: http://goo.gl/bCFfXV

Backpack

Materials

1 skein Red Heart Super Saver worsted weight yarn
Knitting needles size 6mm

Crochet hook
Yarn needle

Directions

Body

Row 1: Cast 85 stitches onto the needle.
Row 2: Knit all the way across.
Row 3: Purl all the way across.
Next rows: Continue working in stockinette stitch until piece measures 14". Bind off.

Bottom

Row 1: Cast 33 stitches onto the needle.
Row 2: Knit all the way across.
Row 3: Purl all the way across.
Next rows: Continue working in stockinette stitch until piece measures 3". Bind off.

Finishing

Drawstring: Crochet a chain measuring 36".

Straps (make 2): With 2 strands of yarn, crochet a chain measuring 34".

Assembly: Fold bag in half and stitch along the side seam. Stitch bottom piece to bag section. Stitch straps to top and bottom at each side of bag. Weave drawstring through top section of bag.

Photo for reference only: http://goo.gl/lGZo8h

ENCIL CASE   August 3

Materials

Yellow, grey, black, beige, and pink worsted weight yarn

4 double pointed knitting needles size 5mm

Directions

Round 1: Cast 18 stitches onto the needle with pink yarn.

Rounds 2-7: Knit all the way around.

Rounds 8-9: Switch to gray yarn, knit all the way around.

Rounds 10-11: Switch to yellow yarn, knit all the way around.

Round 12: Switch to gray yarn, knit all the way around.

Rounds 13-14: *K1, P1. Repeat from * to end of round.

Rounds 15-16: Switch to yellow yarn, knit all the way around.

Rounds 17-18: Switch to gray yarn, knit all the way around.

Round 19: Switch to yellow yarn, knit all the way around.

Round 20: *K2, slip one stitch as if you were going to purl. Repeat from * to end of round.

Next rounds: Repeat rounds 19-20 until piece measures 9".

Next round: Knit all the way around.

Next round: Switch to beige yarn. *K1, slip one stitch as if you were going to purl. Repeat from * to end of round.

Next 2 rounds: Knit all the way around.

Decrease round 1: *K4, K2tog. Repeat from * to end of round.

Round 2 and all even rounds: Knit all the way around.

Round 3: *K3, K2tog. Repeat from * to end of round.

Round 5: *K2, K2tog. Repeat from * to end of round.

Round 7: *K1, K2tog. Repeat from * to end of round.

Round 8: Switch to black yarn. K2tog all the way around.

Round 9: Knit all the way around. Pull yarn tightly through last 3 stitches.

Finishing

Crochet a chain measuring 12" and weave through the eraser section of the pencil case.

Photo for reference only: http://goo.gl/d3drFD

Lacy Bookmark

Materials

No. 20 crochet cotton

Knitting needles size 1.75mm

Directions

Row 1: Cast 68 stitches onto the needle.
Row 2: K7, place a stitch marker, K54, place a stitch marker, K7.
Row 3: With right side facing, K4, P1 TBL, K2, to second marker, K2, P1 TBL, K4.
Row 4: K4, K1 TBL, K2, K to second marker, K2, K1 TBL, K4.
Rows 5-6: Repeat rows 3-4.
Row 7: Repeat row 2. Bind off.

Finishing

Add a fringe to each end of the bookmark.

Photo for reference only: http://goo.gl/IObyzT

Chunky Boot Cuffs

Materials

Chunky or bulky yarn
Knitting needles size 6.5mm

Yarn needle

Directions

Row 1: Cast 40 stitches onto the needle.
Row 2: *K2, P2. Repeat from * to end of row.
Rows 3-9: Repeat row 2.
Row 10: Knit all the way across.
Row 11: Purl all the way across.
Rows 12-29: Repeat rows 10-11. Bind off.

Finishing

Fold in half and stitch the seam. Turn right side out.

Photo for reference only: https://goo.gl/QNfmGU

Knitted Necklace

Materials

Scraps of cotton yarn
Knitting needles size 6.5mm
4 8mm jump rings

1 necklace clasp
2 9" pieces of chain
2 ribbon end clamps

Directions

Row 1: Cast 16 stitches onto the needle.
Rows 2-10: Purl all the way across. Bind off.

Finishing

Attach ribbon end clamps to either end of the knitted piece. Attach chain to ribbon clamps and clasp with jump rings.

Photo for reference only: http://goo.gl/HSU3li

Bow Ring August 7

Materials

Worsted weight yarn
Knitting needles size 6mm

Adjustable ring
Glue gun and glue

Directions

Row 1: Cast 10 stitches onto the needle.
Rows 2-6: Knit all the way across. Bind off.

Finishing

Wrap a piece of scrap yarn around the middle of the knitted piece several times to create the "knot" in the bow. Glue bow to adjustable ring.

Photo for reference only: http://goo.gl/h6BnwJ

Braided Bangle August 8

Materials

Worsted weight yarn
Knitting needles size 6mm

Bracelet clasp

Directions

Make 3

Row 1: Cast 3 stitches onto the needle.
Row 2: Work an I-cord pattern until piece measures 10". Bind off.

Finishing

Braid the 3 I-cords, tie each end in a knot. Tie each end to the bracelet clasp pieces.

Photo for reference only: http://goo.gl/nfxkkj

Little Girl's Leg Warmers

Materials

1 skein Red Heart Super Saver worsted weight yarn
Double pointed knitting needles size 4mm and 5mm

Directions

Pattern written in a size for pre-schoolers. Larger sizes are in brackets.

Round 1: Cast 36 (40, 44, 48) stitches evenly onto the smaller needles.

Round 2: *K2, P2. Repeat from * to end of round.

Next rounds: Repeat round 2 until piece measures 2.5" (2.5, 3, 3).

Next rounds: Switch to larger needles, and work in stockinette stitch until piece measures 8.5" (10, 12.5, 14.5).

Next rounds: Switch to smaller needles. Repeat round 2 for 2.5 (2.5, 3, 3) inches. Bind off.

Photo for reference only: http://goo.gl/5yah1Z

Swirly Coasters

Materials

Worsted weight yarn
3 double pointed knitting needles size 3.75mm
Yarn needle

Directions

Row 1: Cast 3 stitches onto the needle.

Row 2: Work I-cord pattern until piece measures 36". Bind off.

Finishing

Wrap I-cord in a flat spiral pattern. Stitch to secure.

Photo for reference only: http://goo.gl/f02U8V

Swiffer Mop Cover

Materials

Worsted weight yarn
Knitting needles size 4.5mm

Yarn needle

Directions

Main section

Row 1: Cast 42 stitches onto the needle.

Row 2: With right side facing, knit all the way across.
Rows 3-4: Purl all the way across.
Row 5: Knit all the way across.
Next rows: Repeat rows 2-5 until piece measures 4". Bind off.

Sides (make 2)

Row 1: Cast 14 stitches onto the needle.
Next rows: Repeat rows 2-5 of main piece until piece measures 4". Bind off.

Finishing

Stitch side pieces to either end of the main piece.

Photo for reference only: http://goo.gl/e4Zd1o

PRON   August 12

Materials

1 skein worsted weight yarn   Crochet hook
Knitting needles size 6mm

Directions

Row 1: Cast 40 stitches onto the needle.
Row 2: Knit all the way across.
Row 3: K4, P to last 4 stitches, K4.
Next rows: Repeat rows 2-3 until piece measures 14". Bind off.

Finishing

Attach crochet hook at top corner of apron and crochet a chain measuring 18". Repeat on other side.

Photo for reference only: http://goo.gl/VUqeyp

BANGLE BRACELET   August 13

Materials

8-ply DK weight yarn
3 double pointed knitting needles size 3.25mm

Directions

Round 1: Cast 48 stitches onto the needles evenly.
Round 2: Knit all the way around.
Next rounds: Repeat round 2 until piece measures 1.25". Bind off.

Finishing

Allow piece to roll up naturally into a tube shape. Stitch ends together.

Photo for reference only: http://goo.gl/hsTMV0

CHOKER

Materials

8-ply DK weight yarn
3 double pointed knitting needles size 3.25mm
Necklace clasp

Directions

Round 1: Cast 95 stitches onto the needles evenly.
Round 2: Knit all the way around.
Next rounds: Repeat round 2 until piece measures 1.25". Bind off.

Finishing

Allow piece to roll up naturally into a tube shape. Tie ends to necklace clasp pieces.

Photo for reference only: http://goo.gl/z9xuWc

BOW TIE

Materials

Worsted weight yarn
Knitting needles size 6mm

Ribbon
Needle and thread

Directions

Row 1: Cast 14 stitches onto the needle.
Row 2: Knit all the way across.
Next rows: Repeat row 2 until piece measures 2".
Next row: K2tog to end of row.
Next row: Knit all the way across.
Next row: KFBL to end of row.
Next rows: Knit all the way across until section measures 2". Bind off.

Finishing

Wrap yarn around middle section several times to create a "knot" in the bow. Run ribbon through back of knot, and tie around neck.

Photo for reference only: http://goo.gl/5HEE9h

BOW NECKLACE

Materials

Worsted weight yarn
Knitting needles size 6mm
2-9" chains

Necklace clasp
4 jump rings
Needle and thread

Directions

Row 1: Cast 14 stitches onto the needle.
Row 2: Knit all the way across.
Next rows: Repeat row 2 until piece measures 2".
Next row: K2tog to end of row.
Next row: Knit all the way across.
Next row: KFBL to end of row.
Next rows: Knit all the way across until section measures 2". Bind off.

Finishing

Wrap yarn around middle section several times to create a "knot" in the bow and secure. Attach chains to each side of the bow with jump rings, and then attach clasp.

Photo for reference only: http://goo.gl/IW04U4

CELL PHONE COZY   August 17

Materials

Worsted weight yarn, 2 colors
3 double pointed knitting needles size
   3.75

Button
Needle and thread
Yarn needle

Directions

Round 1: Cast 24 stitches evenly onto the needles with main color.
Round 2: Knit all the way around.
Next rounds: Repeat round 2 until piece is long enough to cover your cell phone. Bind off. Turn inside out, and stitch bottom seam.
Flap row 1: Measure 1" down from top of knitted piece, and pick up center 7 stitches. Knit all the way across.
Next rows: Knit all the way across. Repeat until flap measures about 3". Bind off.

Finishing

Stitch button onto the front of cozy.

Photo for reference only: http://goo.gl/VxKNkL

BUTTONS   August 18

Materials

Worsted weight yarn
Knitting needles size 4mm
Yarn needle

Directions

Row 1: Cast 15 stitches onto the needle.
Row 2: Cast off.

Finishing

Thread tail through yarn needle, and roll knitted piece into a tight ball. Stitch to secure and tie the 2 ends into a knot.

Photo for reference only: http://goo.gl/N3Y6gy

Beer Bottle Cozy   August 19

Materials

Worsted weight yarn   Yarn needle
Knitting needles size 3.75mm

Directions

Row 1: Cast 30 stitches onto the needle.
Row 2: Purl all the way across.
Row 3: Knit all the way across.
Row 4: Purl all the way across.
Row 5: Knit all the way across.
Row 6: Purl all the way across.
Row 7: Knit all the way across.
Rows 8-25: Repeat rows 2-7.
Row 26: Purl all the way across.
Row 27: Knit all the way across.
Row 28: Purl all the way across. Bind off.

Finishing

Fold in half with right sides together. Stitch seam and turn right side out.

Photo for reference only: http://goo.gl/D76rWh

Steering Wheel Cover   August 20

Materials

Worsted weight yarn   Yarn needle
Knitting needles size 4mm

Directions

Row 1: Cast 10 stitches onto the needle.
Row 2: Knit all the way across.
Row 3: Repeat row 2 until piece measures 32". Bind off.

Finishing

Wrap around steering wheel and whip stitch all the way around.

Photo for reference only: http://goo.gl/QYNkhf

Easy Belt   August 21

Materials

Chunky yarn   Knitting needles size 5mm

Directions

Row 1: Cast 14 stitches onto the needle.
Row 2: SL1 knitwise, P1. *K1, P1. Repeat from * to end of row.
Row 3: Repeat row 2 until piece reaches desired length. Bind off.

Photo for reference only: http://goo.gl/kppzH0

Hair Tie   August 22

Materials

Worsted weight yarn   Knitting needles size 4.5mm

Directions

Make 2
Row 1: Cast 3 stitches onto the needle.
Row 2: P3.
Row 3: K1, YO, K1, YO, K1.
Row 4: Purl to end of row.
Row 5: K1, YO, K to last stitch, YO, K1.
Row 6: Purl to end of row.
Next rows: Repeat rows 5-6 until piece reaches desired width.
Next rows: Purl all even rows. Right side rows: K1, YO, K2tog, K to last 3 stitches, K2tog, YO, K1. Repeat these 2 rows until piece is 24". Bind off.

Finishing

Stitch both pieces together at straight edge.

Photo for reference only: http://goo.gl/O3nOct

"Diamond" Ring

Materials

Worsted weight yarn, yellow and white
2 double pointed knitting needles size
2.25mm

Directions

Row 1: Cast 3 stitches onto the needle.
Row 2: Knit an I-cord 1" in length.
Diamond row: Still doing the I-cord stitch, K1. With yellow yarn, K1, YO, K1, YO, K1 (all in second stitch). Turn. P5, turn. K5, turn. P2tog, P1, P2tog TBL, turn. K3tog. K1 with MC. Do another inch of I-cord to finish the ring.

Finishing

Stitch ends together to form the ring section.

Photo for reference only: http://goo.gl/L9iqsn

Earrings 1

Materials

2 spools 32 gauge silver color wire
8 pearl beads, 2.5mmX4mm
2 silver cable thimbles or wire guardian

1 pair French earring wires, silver
Knitting needles size 2.75mm
Wire cutters

Directions

Make 2
Pre-string 4 beads onto the wire.
Row 1: Cast 5 stitches onto the needle.
Row 2: (K1, place bead) 4 times, K1.
Rows 3-8: K all stitches.
Row 9: SSK, K1, K2tog.
Rows 10-12: K all stitches. Trim wire but don't cast off.

Finishing

Thread wire through remaining stitches and through cable thimble, then repeat the process. Wrap tail around top of piece and wrap wire around a couple of times to secure. Attach earring hooks.

Photo for reference only: http://goo.gl/LonmYH

Materials

2 spools 32 gauge silver color wire
44 pearl beads, 2.5mm X 4mm
2 silver plated cable thimbles

1 pair silver earring hooks
Knitting needles size 2.75mm
Wire cutters

Directions

Make 2
Pre-string 22 beads onto the wire.
Row 1: Cast 8 stitches onto the needle.
Rows 2-3: (K1, place bead) 7 times, K1.
Rows 4-6: K all stitches.
Row 7: SSK, Kr, K2tog.
Row 8: K all stitches.
Row 9: (K1 place bead) 5 times, K1.
Row 10: K all stitches.
Row 11: SSK, K2, K2tog.
Row 12: (K1, place bead) 3 times, K1.

Finishing

Cut wire with a 4" tail. Thread through remaining live stitches and cable thimble, then repeat the process. Wrap tail around top of piece a couple of times to secure. Trim wire. Connect earring hooks.

Photo for reference only: http://goo.gl/mkV3Ej

Materials

2 spools 32 gauge silver color wire
32 pearl beads (2.5mm X 4mm)
2 silver cable thimbles

2 silver earring hooks
Knitting needles size 2.75mm
Wire cutters

Directions

Make 2
Pre-string 16 beads onto the wire
Row 1: Cast 6 stitches onto the needle.
Row 2: K1, place bead, (K2, place bead) twice, K1.
Row 3 and all uneven rows: K all stitches.
Row 4: K2, (place bead, K2) twice.
Row 6: Repeat row 2.
Row 8: Repeat row 4.
Row 10: Repeat row 2.

Row 12: SSK, place bead, K2, place bead, K2tog.
Row 14: SSK, place bead, K3tog.
Row 15: K2.

Finishing

Trim wire and thread tail through live stitches and cable thimble, then repeat the process. Wrap tail around top of piece a couple of times to secure. Attach earring hooks.

Photo for reference only: http://goo.gl/BT4t2D

ABLET COVER August 27

Materials

1 skein worsted weight yarn
Circular knitting needle size 4.5mm

Yarn needle

Directions

Flap Row 1: Work back and forth and not in rounds. Cast 36 stitches onto the needle.
Row 2: Knit all the way across.
Rows 3-35: Knit all the way across. At the end of row 35, cast on 36 stitches and join.
Main section rows 1-4: Knit all the way around.
Round 5: *K4, K1T. Repeat from * to last 2 stitches, K2.
Rounds 6-7: Knit all the way around.
Round 8: *K1, K1T, K3. Repeat from * to last stitch, K1.
Rounds 9-10: Knit all the way around.
Next rounds: Repeat rounds 5-10 4 times.
Next rounds: Repeat round 1 twice. Bind off.

Finishing

Mark piece at flap, and fold in half to flap. Stitch side seams. Make 2 I-cords that are 8". Attach 1 to center of cast off row, and 1 to center of cast on row.

Photo for reference only: http://goo.gl/slWBM7

AIR BOWS August 28

Materials

Worsted weight yarn

Knitting needle size 4mm

Directions

Row 1: Cast 70 stitches onto the needle.
Row 2: Knit all the way across. Cast off.

Finishing

Tie cord into a bow.

Photo for reference only: http://goo.gl/iblNkv

$\mathcal{T}$RIANGLE PENDANT   **August 29**

Materials

Sock yarn
Knitting needles size 3.25mm

Chain
Jump ring

Directions

Row 1: Cast 8 stitches onto the needle with 2 strands.
Row 2: K8.
Row 3: Slip slip K, K4, K2tog.
Row 4: K all stitches.
Row 5: Ssk, K2, K2tog.
Row 6: K all stitches.
Row 7: Ssk, K2tog.
Row 8: K2tog. Pull yarn through last stitch.

Finishing

Place the jump ring at the top of the triangle, run chain through jump ring.

Photo for reference only: http://goo.gl/NfXRVV

$\mathcal{S}$IMPLE DISHCLOTH   **August 30**

Materials

Worsted weight cotton yarn   Knitting needles size 5mm

Directions

Row 1: Cast 37 stitches onto the needle.
Row 2: *K1, yarn in front, SL1, yarn in back. Repeat from * to last stitch, K1.
Row 3: K1, P to last stitch, K1.
Row 4: K1. *K1, yarn in front, SL1, yarn in back. Repeat from * to last stitch, K1.
Row 5: K1, P to last stitch, K1.x
Next rows: Repeat rows 2-5 until piece is square. Bind off.

Photo for reference only: http://goo.gl/Z8iVE5

# BATHROOM MAT

Materials

2 skeins Red Heart Super Saver worsted weight yarn
Knitting needles size 9mm

Directions

Row 1: Cast 52 stitches onto the needle with 2 strands of yarn.
Rows 2-6: Knit all the way across.
Row 7: K2, P1. *K4, P3. Repeat from * 5 times, K4, P1, K2.
Row 8: K3. *P4, K3. Repeat from * 5 times, P4, K3.
Rows 9-12: Repeat rows 7-8.
Row 13: K2, P1. *CF, P3, K4, P3. Repeat from * twice, CF, P1, K2.
Row 14: K3. *P4, K3. Repeat from * 5 times, P4, K3.
Rows 15-18: Repeat rows 13-14.
Rows 19-22: Repeat rows 7-8.
Row 23: K2, P1. *K4, P3, CF, P3. Repeat from * twice, K4, P1, K2.
Row 24: K3. *P4, K3. Repeat from * 5 times, P4, K3.
Rows 25-28: Repeat rows 13-14.
Next rows: Repeat rows 7-28 twice.
Next row: K2, P1. *K4, P3. Repeat from * 5 times, K4, P1, K2.
Next row: K3. *P4, K3. Repeat from * 5 times, P4, K3.
Next 2 rows: Repeat last 2 rows.
Next 5 rows: Knit all the way across. Bind off.

Photo for reference only: http://goo.gl/ktuHbR

TEACHING KIDS TO KNIT

It is really sad that there is not a lot of emphasis put on home economics in schools these days. When these classes were taught regularly, girls and boys were learning how to do a lot of things that would help them later on in life when they would be out on their own. It's high time that kids were taught these skills again, including knitting. These days, a lot of kids might look at you like you are crazy if you offer to teach them to knit. But, most kids do enjoy arts and crafts, and if you approach it right, they will just look at this as another fun craft to learn.

What is the Best Age to Start Teaching Kids to Knit?

A lot of kids will actually take to knitting like ducks to water, as long as you introduce the art to them at the right time. Many people say that they have taught their kids to knit by the time they are six years old, but this may be a bit young. Kids at that age don't have the hand-eye coordination needed for knitting, nor do they have long attention spans. Many people say that eight or nine years of age is a good time to start teaching kids to knit, because they have better hand-eye coordination at this age, and they are better able to sit still for long periods of time.

Don't Force It

Just because you love to knit, it doesn't necessarily mean that your kids are going to love it too. Some kids love it, and others don't. If you start teaching your kids to knit, and they decide that they are not interested, don't force the issue. Instead, wait until they are interested and then offer to teach them. If you force it on them, they will end up hating it, and they won't want to continue learning.

Starting Out

When teaching kids to knit, lessons will depend on their age. If you are teaching younger children, it is best to start out by teaching them how to finger-knit. They can start with two fingers, and work up to all four fingers on one hand once they start to get the hang of it. Then, they can move on to real knitting needles. You may also want to teach them how to use a knitting loom. You can find kids' knitting sets that have various looms that are easy to use, with instructions for all kinds of fun projects.

Keep it Simple

Make sure that you keep the knitting projects simple in the beginning. If they are too complicated, your kids are likely going to lose interest pretty quickly. A great first project is a garter stitch scarf made on large needles with chunky yarn. It is easy to make, and because of the large needles and chunky yarn, it will knit up quickly. Other simple projects for beginner knitters include doll blankets and pillows, simple doll clothes, headbands, hair accessories, etc.

September

This month is devoted to even more specialty knitting stitches that will get you well on your way to becoming a master knitter. Remember, the more stitches you learn, the more fun you are going to have working on all kinds of different patterns. Don't forget to save your practice squares for the afghan project at the end of the year.

KNITTING A SCALLOPED SHELL September 1

Materials
Worsted weight yarn
Knitting needles for the project you are working on

Directions
Row 1: Cast 21 stitches onto the needle.
Row 2: With right side facing, knit all the way across.
Row 3: Purl all the way across.
Rows 4-5: Knit all the way across.
Row 6: *k1, (YO, K1) twice, (double YO) 5 times, (K1, YO) twice. Repeat from * to last stitch, K1.
Row 7: *K5, yarn in front SL 5 purlwise (dropping extra YO), K4. Repeat from * to last stitch, K1.
Row 8: *K5, yarn in back SL 5 purlwise, K4. Repeat from * to last stitch, K1.
Row 9: *P5, P5tog, P4. Repeat from * to last stitch, K1.
Next rows: Repeat rows 2-9 until piece is square. Bind off.

Photo for reference only: http://goo.gl/wiODMK

SCALLOPED SHELL SCARF September 2

Materials
1 skein Red Heart Super Saver worsted weight yarn
Knitting needles size 6mm

Directions
Row 1: Cast 71 stitches onto the needle.
Next rows: Follow rows 2-9 of scalloped shell pattern until piece reaches desired length. Bind off.

Photo for reference only: http://goo.gl/qX7pQY

KNITTING EYELET RIDGES September 3

Materials
Worsted weight yarn
Knitting needles for the project you are working on

Directions
Row 1: Cast 15 stitches onto the needle.
Row 2: With right side facing, knit all the way across.
Rows 3 and 5: Knit all the way across.
Row 4: *K2tog, YO. Repeat from * to last stitch, K1.

Rows 6-15: Work in stockinette stitch.
Next rows: Repeat rows 2-15 until piece is square. Bind off.

Photo for reference only: http://goo.gl/OBcchp

Eyelet Ridge Dishcloth   September 4

Materials

Cotton worsted weight yarn   Knitting needles size 6mm

Directions

Row 1: Cast 33 stitches onto the needle.
Next rows: Follow rows 2-15 of eyelet ridge pattern until piece is square. Bind off.

Photo for reference only: http://goo.gl/NHYd3M

Knitting Tiny Herringbone Stitches   September 5

Materials

Worsted weight yarn   Knitting needles for the pattern you are
                                           working on

Directions

Right twist (RT) – Skip 1 stitch, K in second stitch, K skipped stitch, SL both stitches from needle together.

Left twist (LT) – Skip 1 stitch, pass behind this stitch, K in second stitch through back loop, K skipped stitch in front loop, SL both stitches from needle together.

Row 1: Cast 18 stitches onto the needle.
Row 2: With right side facing, K to last stitch, SL1.
Row 3: P to last stitch, SL1.
Row 4: K1. *RT, LT. Repeat from * to last stitch, SL1.
Row 5: Repeat row 3.
Next rows: Repeat rows 4-5.
Next rows: Repeat all rows until piece is square. Bind off.

Photo for reference only: http://goo.gl/Q65WK2

Tiny Herringbone Placemat   September 6

Materials

Worsted weight yarn
Knitting needles size 6.5mm

Directions

Row 1: Cast 72 stitches onto the needle.

Next rows: Work rows in tiny herringbone stitch pattern until piece is a rectangle and placemat size. Bind off.

Photo for reference only: http://goo.gl/uerDoi

KNITTING SIMPLE EYELET   September 7

Materials

Worsted weight yarn

Knitting needles for the project you are working on

Directions

Row 1: Cast 15 stitches onto the needle.

Rows 2 and 6: With right side facing, knit all the way across.

Row 3 and all wrong side rows: Purl all the way across.

Row 4: K1. *K2tog, YO, K2. Repeat from * to last 2 stitches, K2.

Row 8: K1. *K2, ssk, YO. Repeat from * to last 2 stitches, K2.

Row 9: Purl all the way across.

Next rows: Repeat rows 2-9 until piece is square. Bind off.

Photo for reference only: http://goo.gl/5pvYX7

SIMPLE EYELET SCARF   September 8

Materials

1 skein Red Heart Super Saver worsted weight yarn

Knitting needles size 5.5mm

Directions

Row 1: Cast 71 stitches onto the needle.

Rows 2-5: Knit all the way across.

Next rows: Work rows 2-9 in simple eyelet pattern until piece reaches desired length, beginning and ending with K4.

Next 4 rows: Knit all the way across. Bind off.

Finishing

Add a fringe to each end of the scarf.

Photo for reference only: http://goo.gl/7OfGId

Knitting an Oat Stitch

Materials

Worsted weight yarn

Knitting needles for the project you are working on

Directions

Row 1: Cast 18 stitches onto the needle.

Rows 2, 4, and 6: With wrong side facing, P2. *(K into back and front of stitch) twice, P2. Repeat from * to end of row.

Rows 3, 5, and 7: K2. *(P2tog) twice, K2. Repeat from * to end of row.

Rows 8, 10, and 12: (K into back and front of stitch) twice. *P2, (K into back and front of stitch) twice. Repeat from * to end of row.

Rows 9, 11, and 13: (P2tog) twice. *K2, (P2tog) twice. Repeat from * to end of row.

Next rows: Repeat rows 2-13 until piece is square. Bind off.

Photo for reference only: http://goo.gl/v4CS3p

Oat Stitch Washcloth

Materials

Cotton worsted weight yarn

Knitting needles size 6mm

Directions

Row 1: Cast 36 stitches onto the needle.

Next rows: Work rows 2-13 of oat stitch pattern until piece is square. Bind off.

Photo for reference only: http://goo.gl/JSxXBw

Knitting a Wide Rib

Materials

Worsted weight yarn

Knitting needles for the project you are working on

Directions

Row 1: Cast 15 stitches onto the needle.

Row 2: With right side facing, P5. *K5, P5.

Row 3: K5. *P5, K5.

Next rows: Repeat rows 2-3 until piece is square. Bind off.

Photo for reference only: http://goo.gl/HKk6Qv

WIDE RIB SCARF

Materials

1 skein Red Heart Super Saver worsted weight yarn

Knitting needles size 6mm

Directions

Row 1: Cast 75 stitches onto the needle.

Next rows: Work rows 2-3 of wide rib pattern until piece reaches desired length. Bind off.

Finishing

Add a fringe to each end of the scarf.

Photo for reference only: http://goo.gl/WkzJuU

KNITTING A QUILTED REVERSE STOCKINETTE PATTERN

Materials

Worsted weight yarn

Knitting needles for the pattern you are working on

Directions

Row 1: Cast 15 stitches onto the needle.

Row 2: With right side facing, K1. *SL1, K4, Pass 1t stitch over the 4 K stitches, P3. Repeat from * to last stitch, K1.

Row 3: K1, P1. *K1, K1 stitch under running thread between stitch just knitted and next stitch, K1, P5. Repeat from * to last 2 stitches, P1, K1.

Row 4: K2. *P3, K5. Repeat from * to last 5 stitches, P3, K2.

Row 5: K1, P1. *K3, P5. Repeat from * to last 5 stitches, K3, P1, K1.

Row 6: K2. *3, yarn in back SL1, K4 pass slipped stitch over 4 knitted stitches. Repeat from * to last 5 stitches, P3, K2.

Row 7: K1. *P5, K1, K1 under running thread, K1. Repeat from * to last 6 stitches, P5, K1.

Row 8: K1. *K5, P3. Repeat from * to last 6 stitches, K6.

Row 9: K1. *P5, K3. Repeat from * to last 6 stitches, P5, K1.

Next rows: Repeat rows 2-9 until piece is square. Bind off.

Photo for reference only: http://goo.gl/7bmLD9

Q UILTED REVERSE STOCKINETTE SCARF September 14

Materials

1 skein Red Heart Super Saver worsted weight yarn

Knitting needles size 7mm

Directions

Row 1: Cast 71 stitches onto the needle.

Next rows: Work rows 2-9 of quilted reverse stockinette pattern until piece reaches desired length. Bind off.

Finishing

Add a fringe to each end of the scarf.

Photo for reference only: http://goo.gl/Fihd2Y

K NITTING A BUTTERFLY STITCH September 15

Materials

Worsted weight yarn

Knitting needles for the project you are working on

Directions

Row 1: Cast 19 stitches onto the needle.

Rows 2, 4, 6, 8, and 10 (right side): K2. *Yarn in front, SL5, K5. Repeat from *, end with yarn in front, SL5, K2.

Row 11: P4. *Insert left needle down through the 5 loose strands below the next stitch, P the 5 strands together with next stitch on needle, P9. Repeat from * to end of last 4 stitches, P4.

Rows 12, 14, 16, 18, and 20: K7. *Yarn in front, SL5, K5. Repeat from *, ending with yarn in front, SL5, K7.

Rows 13, 15, 17, and 19: Purl all the way across.

Row 21: P9. *Insert left needle down through the 5 loose strands below the next stitch, P the 5 strands together with the next stitch on needle, P9. Repeat from * to end of row.

Next rows: Repeat rows 2-21 until piece is square. Bind off.

Photo for reference only: http://goo.gl/vHrscc

B UTTERFLY STITCH DISHCLOTH September 16

Materials

Cotton worsted weight yarn
Knitting needles size 5mm

Directions

Row 1: Cast 37 stitches onto the needle.

Rows 2-5: Knit all the way across.

Rows 6 and 8: With right side facing, K1. *K2tog, YO, K1, YO, SL1, K1, PSSO, K3. Repeat from * to last repeat, K1 instead of K3.

Rows 7 and 9: P3. *SL1, P7. Repeat from *, end last repeat with P3 instead of P7.

Rows 10 and 12: K5. *K2tog, YO, K2, SL1, K1, PSSO, K3. Repeat from * to last 2 stitches, K2.

Rows 11 and 13: P7. *SL1, P7. Repeat from * to end of row.

Next rows: Repeat rows 2-13 until piece measures 8-10".

Next 4 rows: Knit all the way across. Bind off.

Photo for reference only: http://goo.gl/LKsgGK

Knitting a Horseshoe Crab Pattern   September 17

Materials

Worsted weight yarn

Knitting needles for the project you are working on

Directions

Row 1: Cast 15 stitches onto the needle.

Row 2: With right side facing, K1, K2tog, YO. *K2, YO, K1, SL-K2tog-PSSO, K1, YO, SL1-K2tog-PSSO, YO. Repeat from * to last 12 stitches, K2, YO, K1, SL1-K2tog-PSSO, K1, YO, K2, YO, SKP, K1.

Row 3: Purl all the way across.

Row 4: K1, K2tog, YO. *K3, YO, SL1-K2-PSSO, YO. Repeat from * to last 6 stitches, K3, YO, SKP, K1.

Next rows: Repeat rows 2-4 until piece is square. Bind off.

Photo for reference only:
http://goo.gl/sIdo0v

Horseshow Crab Scarf   September 18

Materials

1 skein Red Heart Super Saver worsted weight yarn

Knitting needles size 6.5mm

Directions

Row 1: Cast 75 stitches onto the needle.

Next rows: Work rows 2-4 of horseshoe crab pattern until piece reaches desired length. Bind off.

Finishing

Add a fringe to each end of the scarf.

Photo for reference only: http://goo.gl/peyCTw

Knitting a Rib and Welt Pattern

Materials

Worsted weight yarn

Knitting needles for the project you are working on

Directions

Row 1: Cast 16 stitches onto the needle.
Row 2: With right side facing, *K1, P1, K1, P5. Repeat from * to end of row.
Row 3 and all uneven rows: K the K stitches and P the P stitches.
Row 4: K1, P1. *K5, P1, K1, P1. Repeat from * to last 6 stitches, K5, P1.
Row 6: K1. *P5, K1, P1, K1. Repeat from * to last 7 stitches, P5, K1, P1.
Row 8: *K5, P1, K1, P1. Repeat from * to end of row.
Row 10: P4. *K1, P1, K1, P5. Repeat from * to last 4 stitches, (K1, P1) twice.
Row 12: K3. *P1, K1, P1, K5. Repeat from * to last 5 stitches, P1, K1, P1, K2.
Row 14: P2. *K1, P1, K1, P5. Repeat from * to last 6 stitches, K1, P1, K1, P3.
Row 16: K1. *P1, K1, P1, K5. Repeat from * to last 7 stitches, P1, K1, P1, K4.
Row 17: Repeat row 3.
Next rows: Repeat rows 2-17 until piece is square. Bind off.

Photo for reference only: http://goo.gl/IoWFrz

Rib and Welt Table Runner

Materials

1 skein Red Heart Super Saver worsted weight yarn

Knitting needles size 6mm

Directions

Row 1: Cast 74 stitches onto the needle.
Next rows: Work rows 2-17 of rib and welt pattern until piece measures 36" or desired length. Bind off.

Finishing

Put a fringe at either end of the table runner.

Photo for reference only: https://goo.gl/9bsk7q

Knitting a Daisy Stitch Pattern

Materials

Worsted weight yarn
Knitting needles for the project you are working on

Directions

Daisy stitch (DS) – P3tog without letting the 3 stitches fall from the left needle, wind yarn around right needle over top and back to the front, P same 3 stitches together and let fall from the needle.

Row 1: Cast 17 stitches onto the needle.
Rows 2 and 4: Knit all the way across.
Row 3: K1. *3DS, K1. Repeat from * to end of row.
Row 5: K1, P1. *3DS, K1. Repeat from * to last 2 stitches, P1, K1.
Next rows: Repeat rows 2-5 until piece is square. Bind off.

Photo for reference only: http://goo.gl/nuOVcM

DAISY STITCH DISHCLOTH   September 22

Materials

Worsted weight cotton yarn   Knitting needles size 6mm

Directions

Row 1: Cast 37 stitches onto the needle.
Rows 2-5: Knit all the way across.
Rows 6-9: K4, follow 1-4 of daisy stitch to last 4 stitches, K4.
Next rows: Repeat rows 6-9 until piece is an inch or so away from being square.
Last 4 rows: Knit all the way across. Bind off.

Photo for reference only: http://goo.gl/V3kLuC

KNITTING A SINGLE BASKET WEAVE PATTERN   September 23

Materials

Worsted weight yarn   Knitting needles for the project you are working

Directions

Row 1: Cast 18 stitches onto the needle.
Row 2: With right side facing, P2. *K1, P1. Repeat from * to end of row.
Row 3: *K3, P1. Repeat from * to last 2 stitches, K2.
Row 4: P2. *K1, P3. Repeat from * to end of row.
Row 5: Repeat row 2.
Row 6: *K1, P3. Repeat from * to last stitch, P1.
Row 7: K1, P1. *K3, P1. Repeat from * to end of row.
Next rows: Repeat rows 2-7 until piece is square. Bind off.

Photo for reference only: http://goo.gl/r1sY5G

SINGLE BASKET WEAVE WASHCLOTH   September 24

Materials

Cotton worsted weight yarn   Knitting needles size 6mm

Directions

Row 1: Cast 38 stitches onto the needle.
Next rows: Work rows 2-7 of single basket weave pattern until piece is square. Bind off.

Photo for reference only: http://goo.gl/2Slwju

KNITTING A DIAGONAL SLIP STITCH PATTERN   September 25

Materials

Worsted weight yarn   Knitting needles for the project you are working on

Directions

Row 1: Cast 17 stitches onto the needle.
Row 2: With wrong side facing, purl all the way across.
Row 3: K1. *SL1, K3. Repeat from * to end of row.
Row 4: *P3, SL1. Repeat from * to last stitch, P1.
Row 5: K1. *Drop next SL stitch off left needle to front of work, K2, pick up dropped stitch and knit it, K1. Repeat from * to end of row.
Row 6: Purl all the way across.
Row 7: K3. *P2, SL1, K1. Repeat from * to last 2 stitches, K2.
Row 8: P2. *P1, SL1, P2. Repeat from * to last 3 stitches, P3.
Row 9: K3. *SL next 2 stitches, drop next SL stitch from left needle to front, place 2 SL stitches back on left needle, pick up dropped stitch and knit it, K3. Repeat from * to last 2 stitches, K2.
Next rows: Repeat rows 2-9 until piece is square. Bind off.

Photo for reference only: http://goo.gl/plg1ZO

DIAGONAL SLIP STITCH SCARF   September 26

Materials

1 skein Red Heart Super Saver worsted weight yarn   Knitting needles size 7mm

Directions

Row 1: Cast 77 stitches onto the needle.
Rows 2-3: Knit all the way across.

Next rows: K2, work diagonal slip stitch pattern, K2. Follow pattern until piece reaches desired length.
Last 2 rows: Knit all the way across. Bind off.

Photo for reference only: http://goo.gl/AKFTCc

Knitting a Jumbo Cable Pattern   September 27

Materials

Worsted weight yarn

Knitting needles for the project you are working on

Directions

Special stitch: 16 stitch LC – SL 8 stitches to cable needle and hold to front, K8, K8 from cable needle.
Row 1: Cast 20 stitches onto the needle.
Row 2: With right side facing, knit all the way across.
Row 3 and all odd rows: Purl all the way across.
Row 4: K2, 16LC, K2.
Rows 6, 8, 10, 12, 14, and 16: Knit all the way across.
Row 17: Repeat row 3.
Next rows: Repeat rows 2-17 until piece is square. Bind off.

Photo for reference only: http://goo.gl/0kphNj

Jumbo Cable Leg Warmers   September 28

Materials

1 skein Red Heart Super Saver worsted weight yarn

4 double pointed knitting needles size 4mm and 5mm

Directions

Make 2
Row 1: Cast 72 stitches evenly onto the smaller needles.
Next rows: *K2, P2. Repeat from * to end of round. Repeat round until ribbing measures 2".
Next rows: Switch to larger needles. *K8, follow jumbo cable pattern. Repeat from * twice. Follow pattern until piece measures 15" from cast on edge.
Next rows: Switch to smaller needles and knit 2 inches of ribbing. Bind off.

Photo for reference only: http://goo.gl/kKt5FJ

Knitting a Little Fountain Pattern   September 29

Materials

Worsted weight yarn

Knitting needles for the project you are working on

Directions

Row 1: Cast 17 stitches onto the needle.
Row 2: With right side facing, K1. *YO, K3, YO, K1. Repeat from * to end of row.
Row 3: Purl all the way across.
Row 4: K2, SL1, K2tog, PSSO. *K3, SL1, K2tog, PSSO. Repeat from * to last 2 stitches, K2.
Row 5: Purl all the way across.
Next rows: Repeat rows 2-5 until piece is square. Bind off.

Photo for reference only: http://goo.gl/jMRJ4w

LITTLE FOUNTAIN PATTERN LEG WARMERS   September 30

Materials

1 skein Red Heart Super Saver worsted weight yarn

4 double pointed knitting needles size 5mm and 6mm

Directions

Make 2
Row 1: Cast 65 stitches evenly onto the smaller needles.
Next rows: Work in ribbing pattern for 3".
Next rows: Work in little fountain pattern until piece measures 15".
Last rows: Work in ribbing until piece measures 18". Bind off.

Photo for reference only: https://goo.gl/hdW107

How to Knit with Beads

Now that you have been working on a lot of different types of knitting projects, it is time to step up your game and add a bit of bling to the items you knit. One of the most fun ways to do this is by knitting with beads. Believe it or not, this is not nearly as difficult as it looks. In fact, there is a tried and true method of beaded knitting that is as easy as straight knitting. Let's take a look at knitting with beads to make your projects really stand out.

Method 1

The first method of knitting with beads involves stringing the beads onto the yarn before you begin knitting. As you are knitting, you will add a bead at specific (or random, depending on your tastes and what you are making) simply by pulling it near the needle and creating a stitch. The bead will automatically be incorporated into that stitch. It is best to start with one color of bead until you are used to knitting with beads. Then, you can take it to the next level and start adding more colors, and even creating patterns with the beads. There are many knitting charts that incorporate beads into the patterns.

Method 2

The second method of knitting with beads is very similar to the first, but you will be using a lot more beads. This method has long been used when making purses and other items that have a lot beadwork. Basically, you will be stringing the beads onto the yarn just as you would for method one. The difference is that instead of picking up a single bead here and there, you will be putting a bead between every stitch. This is going to completely cover the stitches, so all you see is the beadwork. Again, as you get better at it, you can start incorporating more colors and creating patterns with the beads.

Method 3

This doesn't involve knitting with the beads at all, and for some it may be the easiest way to add beads to knitted items. Once you have completed the knitting, simply stitch the beads to the item in whatever pattern you like. The only problem with this method is that it can be incredibly time-consuming.

Best Beads and Yarn to Use in Knitted Projects

The type of yarn you are using will play a big role in the types of beads you will use for your projects. For instance, if you are using a fine yarn, such as silks or metallic, you will want to use beads made from glass, pearl, gemstones, etc. If you are using a rougher yarn, such as wool, wood and plastic beads are often a better option. Another thing to consider is how easy it will be to work with the various beads and yarn. Some yarns are extremely fragile, and are not strong enough for beading. Heavier yarns with heavy beads will make for uncomfortable items that are heavy to wear. Consider the project as well when you are choosing beads and yarn. Also, make sure that the beads can withstand going into the washer and dryer. Otherwise, you will have to hand-wash or dry clean your items that have been knitted with beads.

October

Winter will soon be here, so this month there are loads of patterns for cowls, fingerless gloves, hats, and more. Be sure to check out the many awesome patterns for home décor items, as well as items for cleaning your home and yourself.

Cozy Ear Warmers

Materials

1 skein fleece yarn
Knitting needles size 6.5mm

Yarn needle

Directions

Row 1: Cast 8 stitches onto the needle.
Row 2: Purl all the way across.
Row 3: Knit all the way across.
Next rows: Continue working in stockinette stitch until piece measures 23". Bind off.

Finishing

Fold piece in half and stitch ends together.

Simple 2-Needle Mittens

Materials

1 skein super bulky yarn

Knitting needles size 7.5mm

Directions

Make 2
Row 1: Cast 22 stitches onto the needle.
Rows 2-11: *K1, P1. Repeat from * to end of row.
Row 12: With right side facing, K1. *M1, K2. Repeat from * to last 2 stitches, M1, K1.
Rows 13-19: Work in stockinette stitch.
Row 20: Continuing working in stockinette stitch, M1 on stitch 10 and on stitch 18.
Row 21: M1 on stitch 10 and on stitch 22.
Row 22: K11, place 10 stitches onto a stitch holder K11.
Rows 23-33: Work in stockinette stitch.
Row 34: *K2tog, K3. Repeat from * to end of row.
Row 35: Work in stockinette stitch.
Row 36: *K2tog, K2. Repeat from * to end of row. Pull thread tightly through remaining stitches. Stitch side seam with the exception of the thumb hole.
Thumb rows 1-5: Place stitches on stitch holder back onto the needle, and work in stockinette stitch.
Row 2: *K2tog. Repeat from * to end of row. Pull yarn tightly through remaining stitches, and stitch thumb seam. Turn right side out.

Photo for reference only: http://goo.gl/Ajr6cQ

TEXTURED PATTERN BOOT CUFFS

Materials

Worsted weight yarn
Knitting needles size 5mm

Yarn needle

Directions

Row 1: Cast 74 stitches onto the needle.
Row 2: *K2, P2. Repeat from * to end of row.
Rows 3-13: Repeat row 2.
Row 14: Purl all the way across.
Row 15: Purl all the way across.
Rows 16-18: Work in stockinette stitch.
Row 19: Knit all the way across.
Row 20: Knit all the way across.
Rows 21-23: Work in stockinette stitch.
Rows 24-32: Repeat rows 14-23.
Row 33: P2tog, P2. *P2tog, P2. Repeat from * to end of row. Bind off.

Finishing

Fold piece in half with right sides facing. Stitch seam and turn right side out.

Photo for reference only: http://goo.gl/n0Tm3X

SEED STITCH SCARF

Materials

2 skeins chunky yarn
Knitting needles size 7mm

Yarn needle

Directions

Row 1: Cast 19 stitches onto the needle.
Row 2: *K1, P1. Repeat from * to last stitch, K1.
Row 3: Repeat row 2 until piece reaches desired length. Bind off.

Finishing

Add a fringe at each end of the scarf.

Photo for reference only: http://goo.gl/Sw6wOU

RIDGED SCARF

Materials

2 skeins Red Heart Super Saver worsted weight yarn
Knitting needles size 7mm

Directions

Row 1: Cast 39 stitches onto the needle.
Row 2: *K2, P2. Repeat from * to last 3 stitches, K2, P1.
Next rows: Repeat row 2 until piece reaches desired length. Bind off.

Photo for reference only: http://goo.gl/KDOFR3

TWISTED HEADBAND

Materials

1 skein chunky yarn   Yarn needle
Knitting needles size 9mm

Directions

Row 1: Cast 20 stitches onto the needle.
Row 2: Knit all the way across.
Row 3: Purl all the way across.
Next rows: Continue working in stockinette stitch until piece measures 5". Bind off.

Finishing

Lay piece flat and twist it once. Fold in half, and stitch seam. Turn right side out.

Photo for reference only: http://goo.gl/YZoh7z

KNOTTED HEADBAND

Materials

1 skein worsted weight yarn   Yarn needle
Knitting needles size 6.5mm

Directions

Row 1: Cast 10 stitches onto the needle.
Row 2: *YO, slip first stitch purlwise, K1. Repeat from * to end of row.
Row 3: *YO, SL1 purlwise, K 2 criss-cross stitches together. Repeat from * to end of row.
Row 4: Repeat row 3 until piece measures about 35-40" (long enough to wrap around your head twice less a couple of inches. Bind off.

Finishing

Wrap piece around your head so ends are in front, twist ends, wrap to the back. Pin ends together. Remove from head and stitch seam.

Photo for reference only: http://goo.gl/dzl9yZ

FRINGED SHOULDER BAG   October 8

Materials

1 skein Red Heart Super Saver worsted weight yarn
Knitting needles size 5mm
Pony beads

Yarn needle
Button
Needle and thread

Directions

Row 1: Cast 28 stitches onto the needle.
Rows 2, 4, 7, and 9: P4. *K4, P4. Repeat from * to end of row.
Rows 3, 5, 6, and 8: K4. *P4, K4. Repeat from * to end of row.
Next rows: Repeat rows 2-9 until piece measures 16".
Flap row 1: Working in basket weave pattern, decrease 1 stitch at the beginning of the row.
Rows 2-18: Repeat flap row 1.
Buttonhole row: Continuing basket weave pattern, dec 1, work 3 stitches, YO, dec 1 to end of row.
Next rows: Continue working in basket weave pattern, decreasing 1 stitch at the beginning of each row until there are 3 stitches remaining. Bind off.

Finishing

Knit an I-cord strap that is 24". Mark main piece at flap, and fold in half to flap. Stitch side seams. Stitch button to front of bag. Stitch I-cord to top sides of bag. Add a fringe along bottom of bag, and add beads to the fringes.

Photo for reference only: https://goo.gl/cS9WZ4

BALLERINA LEG WARMERS   October 9

Materials

1 skein Red Heart Super Saver worsted weight yarn

4 double pointed knitting needles, sizes 3.5mm and 4.5mm

Directions

Make 2
Round 1: Cast 64 stitches onto smaller needles.
Round 2: *K2, P2. Repeat from * to end of round.
Next rounds: Repeat round 2 until piece measures 3".

Next round: Switch to larger needles, K to end of round.
Next rounds: Continue knitting until piece measures 12".
Next rounds: Switch back to smaller needles and knit 3" of ribbing. Bind off.

Photo for reference only: http://goo.gl/ZZ0G2f

VARIEGATED LEG WARMERS October 10

Materials

1 skein variegated Red Heart Super Saver worsted weight yarn

4 double pointed knitting needles size 3.5mm

Directions

Make 2
Round 1: Cast 44 stitches onto the needles.
Round 2: *K1, P1. Repeat from * to end of round.
Rounds 3-9: Repeat round 2.
Rounds 10-118: Knit all the way around.
Rounds 119-126: Repeat round 2. Bind off.

Photo for reference only: http://goo.gl/8Qqn5Z

HAIR SCRUNCHY October 11

Materials

4-py worsted weight yarn
Knitting needles size 3.25mm
Yarn needle

Elastic
Needle and thread

Directions

Row 1: Cast 172 stitches onto the needle.
Row 2: Knit all the way across.
Next rows: Repeat row 2 until piece measures 7". Bind off.

Finishing

Fold piece in half lengthwise, and stitch long seam. Thread elastic through, and pull tightly. Sew elastic ends together to secure. Stitch ends of knitted piece together.

Photo for reference only: http://goo.gl/q3c5Zg

Hair Bun Cover

Materials

1 skein sparkly yarn
Knitting needles sizes 5mm, 6mm, and 15mm

Yarn needle
Ribbon

Directions

Row 1: Cast 12 stitches onto the smallest needles.
Row 2: Knit into front and back of each stitch all the way across.
Row 3: Repeat row 2.
Row 4: Change to 6mm needles, knit all the way across.
Row 5: Change to 15mm needles, knit all the way across.
Rows 6-7: Knit all the way across.
Row 8: Change to 6mm needles, knit all the way across.
Row 9: Knit all the way across. Bind off.

Finishing

Fold piece in half and stitch seam. Thread the ribbon through the row made with the largest needles.

Photo for reference only: http://goo.gl/PPt72K

Easy Ladies' Top

Materials

500 yards DK weight yarn
Knitting needles size 5mm

Yarn needle

Directions

Make 2
Row 1: Cast 99 stitches onto the needle.
Row 2: *K1, P1. Repeat from * to end of row.
Row 3: *P1, K1. Repeat from * to end of row.
Next rows: Repeat rows 2-3 until piece measures 2".
Next rows: Knit all the way across. Continue working garter stitch until piece measures 20". Bind off.

Finishing

Place both pieces together, right sides facing. Stitch side seams, leaving space for armholes. Stitch shoulder seams, leaving space for the neck hole.

Photo for reference only: http://goo.gl/RVUCSv

2-Hour Top

Materials

1 skein Red Heart Super Saver worsted weight yarn

Knitting needles size 15mm
Yarn needle

Directions

Make 2
Row 1: Cast 30 stitches onto the needle.
Row 2: Knit all the way across.
Row 3: Purl all the way across.
Next rows: Repeat rows 2-3 until piece measures 20". Bind off.

Finishing

Place both pieces together, right sides facing. Stitch side seams, leaving space for armholes. Stitch shoulder seams, leaving space for the neck hole.

Photo for reference only: http://goo.gl/D7CUYq

Bulky Mat

Materials

2 skeins super chunky yarn

Circular knitting needle size 19mm

Directions

Row 1: Work back and forth instead of in rounds. Cast 49 stitches onto the needle.
Row 2: With wrong side facing, knit all the way across.
Row 3: *K1, SL1. Repeat from * to last stitch, K1.
Next rows: Repeat rows 2 and 3 until piece reaches desired size. Bind off.

Photo for reference only: http://goo.gl/WEY31h

Handbag

Materials

3 100-gram skeins chunky yarn
Knitting needles size 8mm

2 round bag handles
Yarn needle

Directions

Make 2
Row 1: Cast 40 stitches onto the needle with 3 strands of yarn.
Rows 2-41: Knit all the way across. Bind off.
Handle support (make 2)

Row 1: Cast 6 stitches onto the needle with 3 strands of yarn.

Rows 2-5: Knit all the way across.

Row 6: K2tog, K to last 2 stitches, K2tog.

Rows 7-9: Knit all the way across.

Row 10: Increase, K to last stitch, increase.

Rows 11-13: Knit all the way across. Cast off.

Finishing

Stitch bottom and side seams of bag. Attach one end of the handle support to one side of the bag, put handle in place, and stitch the other end to the opposite side. Repeat on other side of bag.

Photo for reference only: http://goo.gl/8Uspr6

Toilet Seat Cover   October 17

Materials

1 skein Red Heart Super Saver worsted weight yarn

Knitting needles size 6mm
Elastic

Directions

Row 1: Cast 23 stitches onto the needle.

Row 2: K1. *P1, K1. Repeat from * to end of row.

Row 3: P1. *K1, P1. Repeat from * to end of row.

Next rows: Repeat rows 2-3, increasing 1 stitch at each end of every third row and every right side row until there are 59 stitches on the needle. Continue working double moss stitch until piece measures 12".

Next rows: Continue working in double moss stitch, decreasing 1 stitch at each end of every right side row until there are 37 stitches. Cast off.

Finishing

Work casing stitch as close to the edge as possible. Thread elastic through casing and stitch ends to secure.

Photo for reference only: http://goo.gl/dU6Qp1

Toilet Mat   October 18

Materials

1 skein Red Heart Super Saver worsted weight yarn
Knitting needles size 6mm

Directions

Row 1: Cast 69 stitches onto the needle.

Row 2: K1. *P1, K1. Repeat from * to end of row.

Row 3: P1. *K1, P1. Repeat from * to end of row.

Row 4: Repeat row 2.
Row 5: Repeat row 3.
Next rows: Repeat rows 2-5 until piece measures 10".
Next row: Follow stitch pattern 22 stitches, cast off 25 stitches, pattern 22 stitches (place these 22 stitches on a stitch holder.
Next rows: Work in same pattern, decrease 1 stitch in each of the next 4 right side rows. Continue pattern until piece measures 20" from cast on edge. Repeat on other side. Bind off.

Photo for reference only: http://goo.gl/4rdiQU

OVEN CLOTH October 19

Materials

100 grams cotton yarn   Knitting needles size 6.5mm

Directions

Row 1: Cast 36 stitches onto the needle.
Row 2: Knit all the way across.
Row 3: Purl all the way across.
Next rows: Repeat rows 2-3 until piece measures 40". Bind off.

Finishing

Lay piece flat, and fold each end back 6". Stitch up the side seams.

Photo for reference only: http://goo.gl/y4bkz8

HOT WATER BOTTLE COVER October 20

Materials

2 skeins worsted weight yarn   Needle and thread
Knitting needles size 4.5mm   Crochet hook
2 buttons

Directions

Make 2
Row 1: Cast 65 stitches onto the needle with 2 strands of yarn.
Row 2: With wrong side facing, purl all the way across.
Row 3: (K1, YFWD, K4, SL1, K2tog, psso-pass slip stitch over, K4, YFWD, K1) 5 times.
Rows 4-5: Repeat rows 2-3 8 times.
Next rows: Repeat rows 2-5 until piece measures 12". Bind off.

Finishing

Stitch both pieces together along sides and bottom with double crochet. Sew buttons on top, about 3" in on either side.

Photo for reference only: http://goo.gl/xmXDdU

$\mathcal{B}$ATH SCRUBBIE October 21

Materials

Worsted weight cotton yarn   Knitting needles size 5mm

Directions

Row 1: Cast 44 stitches onto the needle.
Rows 2-7: Knit all the way across.
Row 8: With right side facing, purl all the way across.
Row 9: *K1, P1, K1. P3tog. Repeat from * to end of row.
Row 10: Purl all the way across.
Row 11: *P3tog, K1, P1, K1. Repeat from * to end of row.
Next rows: Repeat rows 8-11 until piece measures 10".
Next 6 rows: Knit all the way across. Bind off.

Photo for reference only: http://goo.gl/5KWe5E

$\mathcal{B}$ATH PUFF October 22

Materials

Worsted weight cotton yarn   Yarn needle
Knitting needles size 5mm

Directions

Row 1: Cast 20 stitches onto the needle.
Row 2: Knit all the way across.
Row 3: K1, SSK, K13, K1F&B, K1.
Next rows: Repeat rows 2-3 until piece measures 10". Bind off.

Finishing

Fold piece in half and stitch side seam. Weave thread around the top and bottom, pull tight, and tie off.

Photo for reference only: http://goo.gl/EVvMDd

$\mathcal{K}$NITTED BASKET October 23

Materials

Worsted weight yarn   Knitting needles size 5mm

Directions

Base

Row 1: Cast 12 stitches onto the needle with 2 strands of yarn.
Rows 2-13: Knit all the way across. Bind off.

Edge

Row 1: Cast 40 stitches onto the needle.
Rows 2-9: Knit all the way across. Bind off.

Handle

Row 1: Cast 4 stitches onto needle.
Rows 2-37: Knit all the way across. Bind off.

Finishing

Sew edge and base together, attach handle.

Photo for reference only: http://goo.gl/NL08UZ

CATNIP MOUSE October 24

Materials

8-ply worsted weight yarn
Knitting needles size 5mm
Fiberfill stuffing

Catnip
Yarn needle

Directions

Row 1: Cast 18 stitches onto the needle.
Rows 2-15: Work in stockinette stitch.
Row 16: K2, (K2tog, K4) twice, K2tog, K2.
Row 17 and all uneven rows: Purl all the way across.
Row 18: K2, (K2tog, K3) twice, K2tog, K1.
Row 20: (K3, K2tog) twice, K2.
Row 22: K3, K2tog, K2, K2tog, K1.
Row 24: (K1, K2tog) twice, K2tog.
Row 26: (K2tog) 3 times.
Row 28: K3tog. Bind off.

Finishing

Join side seams and fill with fiberfill stuffing and catnip.

Photo for reference only: http://goo.gl/ESCveR

BUCKLED BELT October 25

Materials

Double worsted yarn
Knitting needles size 6mm

Belt buckle
Yarn needle

Directions

Row 1: Cast 10 stitches onto the needle with 2 strands of yarn.
Row 2: Knit all the way across.
Row 3: *K1, P1. Repeat from * to end of row.
Next rows: Repeat rows 2-3 until piece measures 3".
Next row: Knit, increasing 5 stitches evenly across row.
Next rows: Repeat rows 2-3 until piece measures 48". Bind off.

Finishing

Secure buckle in first 3" of belt. Stitch into place.

Photo for reference only: http://goo.gl/EEcvbg

Neck Warmer   October 26

Materials

1 skein worsted weight yarn   Pretty brooch
Knitting needles size 6mm

Directions

Row 1: Cast 12 stitches onto the needle, loosely.
Row 2: K1, P1, K8, P1, K1.
Row 3: K1, P10, K1.
Next rows: Repeat rows 2-3 until piece reaches desired length, less 2".
Next 6 rows: Knit all the way across. Bind off.

Finishing

Use brooch as a clasp to hold neck warmer on.

Photo for reference only: http://goo.gl/KXl0mZ

Flower Brooch   October 26

Materials

Worsted weight yarn   Pin back
Knitting needles size 5mm   Glue gun and glue

Directions

Row 1: Cast 6 stitches onto the needle.
Row 2: Knit in the front and back of each stitch.
Row 3: Knit all the way across.
Row 4: Repeat row 2.
Row 5: Repeat row 3.
Row 6: Repeat row 2.

Row 7: Repeat row 3. Bind off.

Finishing

Shape into a flower by rolling up and pinching at one end, stitch to secure. Glue pin back to back of flower.

Photo for reference only: http://goo.gl/DzxMjy

Knitter's Brooch   October 27

Materials

Worsted weight yarn
Knitting needles size 3.5mm
2 toothpicks

2 5mm pearl beads
Glue gun and glue
Pin back

Directions

Row 1: Cast 10 stitches onto the needle.
Row 2: Knit all the way across.
Rows 3-12: Repeat row 2. Do not bind off.

Finishing

Stick pearl beads on one end of each of the toothpicks, and glue into place. Slide toothpick "knitting needles" onto the knitted piece (5 stitches on each needle), and glue in place. Glue the pin back to the back of the piece.

Photo for reference only: http://goo.gl/VYLR4r

Ruffled Arm Warmers   October 28

Materials

Worsted weight yarn, 2 colors
Knitting needles size 5mm

Yarn needle

Directions

Make 2
Row 1: Cast 60 stitches onto the needle in ruffle color.
Rows 2-7: Work in stockinette stitch, ending on a purl row.
Row 8: Switch to MC, K2tog all the way across.
Rows 9-11: Knit all the way across.
Next rows: Work in stockinette stitch until piece reaches desired length. Bind off.

Finishing

Fold piece in half and stitch up side seam. Turn right side out.

Photo for reference only: http://goo.gl/i9cwEW

UFFLED CANDLE MAT

Materials

Worsted weight yarn
4 double pointed knitting needles size 5mm

Directions

Round 1: Cast 200 stitches evenly onto needles.
Rounds 2-5: Knit all the way around.
Round 6: *K1, drop next stitch. Repeat from * to end of round.
Round 7: SSK around.
Round 8: Knit all the way around.
Round 9: *K3, ssk. Repeat from * to end of round.
Round 10: Knit all the way around.
Round 11: *K2, ssk. Repeat from * to end of round.
Round 12: Knit all the way around.
Round 13: *K1, ssk. Repeat from * to end of round,
Round 14: Knit all the way around.
Round 15: Ssk all the way around. Bind off.

Photo for reference only: https://goo.gl/YKTdba

LATTICE STITCH TABLE RUNNER

Materials

1 skein Red Heart Super Saver worsted   Knitting needles size 5mm
weight yarn

Directions

Lattice pattern

Rows 1 and 3: With wrong side facing, purl all the way across.
Row 2: K2. *YO, K3, lift first stitch of stitches just knitted with left needle over last 2 stitches. Repeat from * to last stitch, K1.
Row 4: K1. *K3, lift first stitch of stitches just knitted with left needle over last 2 stitches. Repeat from * to last 2 stitches, K2.
Rows 5-8: Repeat rows 1-4 of pattern.

Table Runner

Row 1: Cast 70 stitches onto the needle.
Rows 2-11: Knit all the way across.
Row 12: With wrong side facing, K5, place stitch marker, work lattice pattern for 60 stitches, place stitch marker, K5.

Row 13: With right side facing, work row 2 of lattice pattern over 60 stitches, K5.

Next rows: Continue working in lattice pattern until piece is about 40" long, ending with row 4 of pattern.

Next 10 rows: Knit all the way across. Bind off.

Photo for reference only: https://goo.gl/c2Yn92

$\mathcal{J}$ACK-O-LANTERN PIN October 31

Materials

Orange worsted weight yarn
3-4 double pointed knitting needles size 5mm
Yellow, black, and green felt

Pin back
Glue gun and glue
Yarn needle

Directions

Round 1: Cast 3 stitches onto the needle.

Next rounds: Work I-cord pattern until piece reaches 12". Bind off.

Finishing

Curl I-cord into a flat circle, stitch together. Cut out felt pieces for eyes, nose, mouth, and leaf, glue to knitted piece. Glue pin back to the back of knitted piece.

Photo for reference only: https://goo.gl/YDc5ug

How to Knit with a Loom

There are all kinds of fun projects that you can do with knitting looms, and using looms is a great way for kids to learn the joy of knitting. You don't even need to use knitting needles when using a loom. All you need is yarn, a loom, and a knitting or crochet hook for making stitches (some people don't use a hook, but it does make the process a whole lot easier).

Choose a Loom

The first thing you need to do is choose the loom you want to work with. The size of the loom will affect the finished project, so make sure that you choose the right size. You will basically be making a knitted tube, but the loom size will determine the width, and not the length of the finished product. If you are planning on knitting with two different yarn colors, make sure that you don't use thick yarn as you won't be able to work on the loom.

Getting Started

The first thing you need to do is tie the end of your yarn to the hook that is located on the side of the loom. This is going to keep the work anchored in place until you are finished. To do this, make a loop as you would to start any knitting project, and wrap it around the hook. Tie a knot to make sure that it isn't going to slip.

Now, you can start the first row, or "casting on". Using the long end of the yarn, begin wrapping the yarn, clockwise, around each peg of the loom until you have gotten all the way around. Repeat so you have two rows of loops on the pegs. Now, with the knitting hook, grab the bottom loop, and pull it over the top loop and up over the peg. You have created your first stitch. Continue doing this all the way around. You now have all of your stitches cast on the loom. Continue in this manner until the piece reaches the desired length.

Finishing Up

Casting off is a bit more difficult. With one loop on every peg, pull the loop of the second peg, and put it over the peg to the left. Next, pull the bottom loop up and over the top loop, take the loop that is on that peg, and place it on the empty peg. Keep doing this until there is one stitch remaining on the loom. Cut the yarn, pull the tail through the last loop, and voila, you have just finished your first knitting loom project!

November

We have one more month of specialty knitting stitches for you, along with fun and easy patterns you can use to practice those stitches. Keep all of those practice squares for next month, because you are going to need them to make the patchwork afghan at the end of the month.

KNITTING AN OYSTER STITCH PATTERN

Materials

Worsted weight yarn
Knitting needles for the project you are working on

Directions

Cluster stitch (CS) – Pass next 5 stitches onto right needle, dropping extra loops, pass these stitches back to the left needle, working through all 5 stitches.

Row 1: Cast 13 stitches onto the needle.
Row 2: With right side facing, knit all the way across.
Row 3: P1. *(P1, WYT) 4 times, P2. Repeat from * to end of row.
Row 4: K1. *CS, K1, WYT, P1, WYT, K1, WYT, P1, WYT, K1, WYT, K1. Repeat from * to end.
Row 5: P1 *K5 dropping extra loops, P1. Repeat from * to end of row.
Row 6: Knit all the way across.
Row 7: P4. (P1, WYT) 4 times, P1. *P1, (P1, WYT) 4 times, P1. Repeat from * to last 4 stitches, P4.
Row 8: K4, CS. *K1, CS. Repeat from * to last 4 stitches, K4.
Row 9: P4, K5, dropping extra loops. *P1, K5 dropping extra loops. Repeat from * to last 4 stitches, P4.
Next rows: Repeat rows 2-9 until piece is square. Bind off.

Photo for reference only: http://goo.gl/muA3Vm

OYSTER STITCH SCARF

Materials

1 skein Red Heart Super Saver worsted weight yarn
Knitting needles size 6mm

Directions

Row 1: Cast 73 stitches onto the needle.
Next rows: Work in oyster stitch pattern until piece reaches desired length. Bind off.

Finishing

Gather each end of the scarf and make a tassel at each end.

Photo for reference only: http://goo.gl/owzvli

KNITTING A PILLAR OPENWORK PATTERN

Materials

Worsted weight yarn
Knitting needles for the project you are working on

Directions

Row 1: Cast 17 stitches onto the needle.
Row 2: With right side facing, K1. *YO, SL1 purlwise, K2, PSSO the K2. Repeat from * to last stitch, K1.
Row 3: Purl all the way across.
Next rows: Repeat rows 2-3 until piece is square. Bind off.

Photo for reference only: http://goo.gl/n0Phev

Pillar Openwork Pattern Cowl   November 4

Materials

1 skein Red Heart Super Saver worsted weight yarn

Knitting needles size 6mm
Yarn needle

Directions

Row 1: Cast 74 stitches onto the needle.
Row 2: Work rows 2-3 of pillar openwork pattern until piece measures 18". Bind off.

Finishing

Fold piece in half and stitch seam. Turn right side out.

Photo for reference only: http://goo.gl/jK14Jq

Knitting a Mock Cable Eyelet Ribbing Pattern   November 5

Materials

Worsted weight yarn
Knitting needles for the project you are working on

Directions

Row 1: Cast 17 stitches onto the needle.
Row 2: With right side facing, P2. *SL1, K2, PSSO, P2. Repeat from * to end of row.
Row 3: K2. *P1, YRN, P1, K2. Repeat from * to end of row.
Row 4-5: P2. *K3, P2. Repeat from * to end of row.
Next rows: Repeat rows 2-5 until piece is square. Bind off.

Photo for reference only: http://goo.gl/maFa7b

Mock Cable Eyelet Ribbing Pattern Wrap   November 6

Materials

1 skein Red Heart Super Saver worsted weight yarn
Knitting needles size 8mm

Directions

Row 1: Cast 110 stitches onto the needle.
Rows 2-5: Knit all the way across.
Next rows: K4, follow mock cable eyelet ribbing pattern to last 4 stitches, K4. Repeat until piece reaches desired length. Bind off.

Photo for reference only: https://goo.gl/kJ1TAC

KNITTING A PLEAT PATTERN STITCH   November 7

Materials

Worsted weight yarn
Knitting needles for the project you are working on

Directions

Row 1: Cast 16 stitches onto the needle.
Row 2: With right side facing, K1 B. *P1 K2, P1, K1 B. Repeat from * to end of row.
Row 3: P1. *K1, P2, K1, P1. Repeat from * to end of row.
Row 4: K1 B. *P4, K1 B. Repeat from * to end of row.
Row 5: P1. *K4, P1. Repeat from * to end of row.
Next rows: Repeat rows 2-5 until piece is square. Bind off.

Photo for reference only: http://goo.gl/SHK0VE

PLEAT PATTERN STITCH SCARF   November 8

Materials

1 skein Red Heart Super Saver worsted weight yarn
Knitting needles size 6.5mm

Directions

Row 1: Cast 76 stitches onto the needle.
Next rows: Work rows 2-5 of pleat pattern stitch until piece reaches desired length. Bind off.

Finishing

Add a fringe to each end of the scarf.

Photo for reference only: http://goo.gl/Uw0nSr

KNITTING A PUFFED RIBBING PATTERN   November 9

Materials

Worsted weight yarn
Knitting needles for the project you are working on

Directions

Row 1: Cast 17 stitches onto the needle.
Row 2: With right side facing, P2. *YO, K1, yarn to front, P2. Repeat from * to end of row.
Row 3: K2. *P3, K2. Repeat from * to end of row.
Row 4: P2. *K3, P2. Repeat from * to end of row.
Row 5: K2. *P3tog, K2. Repeat from * to end of row.
Next rows: Repeat rows 2-5 until piece is square. Bind off.

Photo for reference only: http://goo.gl/7PC83g

$\mathcal{P}$UFFED RIBBING SKINNY SCARF

Materials

1 skein chunky yarn   Knitting needles size 6mm

Directions

Row 1: Cast 22 stitches onto the needle.
Next rows: Work rows 2-5 of puffed ribbing pattern until piece reaches desired length. Bind off.

Finishing

Gather each end of the scarf and add a tassel to each end.

Photo for reference only: https://goo.gl/K20z8h

$\mathcal{K}$NITTING AN OPEN CHAIN RIBBING PATTERN

Materials

Worsted weight yarn
Knitting needles for the project you are working on

Directions

Row 1: Cast 14 stitches onto the needle.
Row 2: With wrong side facing, K2. *P4, K2. Repeat from * to end of row.
Row 3: P2. *K2tog, YO twice, SL1, K1, PSSO, P2. Repeat from * to end of row.
Row 4: K2. *P1, P into front of first YO, P into back of second YO, P1, K1. Repeat from * to end of row.
Next rows: Repeat rows 2-4 until piece is square. Bind off.

Photo for reference only: http://goo.gl/yLF82x

Open Chain Ribbing Leg Warmers

Materials

1 skein Red Heart Super Saver worsted weight yarn

4 double pointed knitting needles size 5mm and 6mm

Directions

Make 2

Round 1: Cast 68 stitches evenly onto smaller needles.
Round 2: Knit all the way around.
Round 3: Knit all the way around.
Next rounds: Repeat rounds 2-3 until piece measures 3".
Next rounds: Work in open chain ribbing pattern until piece measures 15".
Next rounds: Repeat rounds 2-3 until piece measures 18". Bind off.

Photo for reference only: https://goo.gl/igEsrb

Knitting a Supple Rib Stitch Pattern

Materials

Worsted weight yarn

Knitting needles for the project you are working on

Directions

Row 1: Cast 16 stitches onto the needle.
Row 2: K1. *K next stitch but don't slip to left needle, P same stitch together with the next stitch, K1. Repeat from * to end of row.
Row 3: Purl all the way across.
Next rows: Repeat rows 2-3 until piece is square. Bind off.

Photo for reference only: http://goo.gl/DC2LX9

Supple Rib Stitch Boot Cuffs

Materials

Worsted weight yarn
4 double pointed knitting needles size 6mm

Directions

Round 1: Cast 60 stitches evenly onto the needles.
Round 2: Knit all the way around.
Round 3: Purl all the way around.

Round 4: Knit all the way around.

Next rows: Work rows 2-3 of supple rib stitch pattern until piece measures 4.5".

Next rows: Repeat rows 2-4. Bind off.

Photo for reference only: http://goo.gl/jmPNih

KNITTING AN ASTRAKHAN BOBBLE STITCH PATTERN   November 15

Materials

Worsted weight yarn
Knitting needles for the project you are working on

Directions

Row 1: Cast 15 stitches onto the needle.

Rows 2-7: K2. *YO, K4, P3tog, K4, YO, K1. Repeat from * to last stitch, K1.

Row 8: K1, P2tog. *K4, YO, K1, YO, K4, P3tog. Repeat from * to last 12 stitches, K4, YO, K1, YO, K4, P2tog, K1.

Rows 9-13: Repeat row 8.

Next rows: Repeat rows 2-13 until piece is square. Bind off.

Photo for reference only: http://goo.gl/626Pjz

ASTRAKHAN BOBBLE STITCH PATTERN SCARF   November 16

Materials

1 skein Red Heart Super Saver worsted weight yarn
Knitting needles size 6mm

Directions

Row 1: Cast 75 stitches onto the needle.

Next rows: Work rows 2-13 of Astrakhan bobble stitch pattern until piece reaches desired length. Bind off.

Finishing

Add a fringe to each end of the scarf.

Photo for reference only: http://goo.gl/0O9O7D

KNITTING A BEAD STITCH PATTERN   November 17

Materials

Worsted weight yarn
Knitting needles for the project you are
working on

Directions

Row 1: Cast 14 stitches onto the needle.

Row 2: With right side facing, K1, K2tog, YO, K1, YO, SL1, K1, PSSO. *K2, K2tog, YO, K1, YO, SL1, K1, PSSO. Repeat from * to last stitch, K1.

Row 3: *P2tog through back loop, YRN, P3, YRN, P2tog. Repeat from * to end of row.

Row 4: K1, YO, SL1, K1, PSSO, K1, K2tog, YO. *K2, YO, SL1, K1, PSSO, K1, K2tog, YO. Repeat from * to last stitch, K1.

Row 5: P2, YRN, P3tog, YRN. *P4, YRN, P3tog, YRN. Repeat from * to last 2 stitches, P2.

Next rows: Repeat rows 2-5 until piece is square. Bind off.

Photo for reference only: http://goo.gl/D9jvAW

BEAD STITCH PATTERN COWL   November 18

Materials

300 grams chunky yarn   Circular Knitting needle size 8mm

Directions

Round 1: Cast 60 stitches onto the needle.

Next rounds: Work rounds 2-5 of bead stitch pattern until piece measures 12-14". Bind off.

Photo for reference only: http://goo.gl/DyvAYO

KNITTING A BELL LACE PATTERN   November 19

Materials

Worsted weight yarn   Knitting needles for the project you are working on

Directions

Row 1: Cast 19 stitches onto the needle.

Row 2: With right side facing, K1, P1, K1. *P1 YO, SL1, K2tog, PSSO, yarn to front; (P1, K1) twice. Repeat from * to end of row.

Row 3: P1, K1, P1. *K1, P3, (K1, P1) twice. Repeat from * to end of row.

Rows 4-7: Repeat rows 2-3.

Row 8: K1, K2tog. *Yarn to front, (P1, K1) twice, P1, YO, SL1, K2tog, PSSO. Repeat from * to last 8 stitches yarn to front, (P1, K1) twice, P1, YO, SL1, PSSO, K1.

Row 9: P3. *(K1, P1) twice, K1, P3. Repeat from * to end of row.

Rows 10-13: Repeat rows 8-9.

Next rows: Repeat rows 2-13 until piece is square. Bind off.

Photo for reference only: http://goo.gl/TXmaqD

Bell Lace Lap Blanket

Materials

2 skeins Red Heart Super Saver worsted weight yarn
Circular knitting needle size 6mm

Directions

Row 1: Work back and forth and not in rounds. Cast 195 stitches onto the needle.
Rows 2-6: Knit all the way across.
Next rows: K4, follow bell lace pattern to last 4 stitches, K4. Repeat until piece reaches desired size.
Last 5 rows: Knit all the way across. Bind off.

Photo for reference only: http://goo.gl/ijSqTv

Knitting a Checkerboard Lace Pattern

Materials

Worsted weight yarn
Knitting needles for the project you are working on

Directions

Row 1: Cast 20 stitches onto the needle.
Row 2: With right side facing, K7. *(YO, K2tog) 3 times, K6. Repeat from * to last stitch, K1.
Row 3 and all uneven rows: Purl all the way across.
Row 4: K7. *(K2tog, YO) 3 times, K6. Repeat from * to last stitch, K1.
Row 6: Repeat row 2.
Row 8: Repeat row 4.
Row 10: K1. *(YO, K2tog) 3 times, K6. Repeat from * to last 7 stitches, (YO, K2tog) 3 times, K1.
Row 12: K1, (K2tog, YO) 3 times. *K6, (K2tog, YO) 3 times. Repeat from * to last stitch, K1.
Row 14: Repeat row 10.
Row 16: Repeat row 12.
Row 17: Purl all the way across.
Next rows: Repeat rows 2-17 until piece is square. Bind off.

Photo for reference only: http://goo.gl/GfVngr

Checkerboard Lace Washcloth

Materials

Cotton worsted weight yarn
Knitting needles size 5.5mm

Directions

Row 1: Cast 44 stitches onto the needle.

Rows 2-3: Knit all the way across.

Next rows: K2, follow checkerboard lace pattern to last 4 stitches, K2. Repeat until piece is square.

Last 2 rows: Knit all the way across.

Photo for reference only: http://goo.gl/kk3JeI

KNITTING A DEWDROP PATTERN   November 23

Materials

Worsted weight yarn

Knitting needles for the project you are working on

Directions

Row 1: Cast 13 stitches onto the needle.

Row 2: With wrong side facing, K2. *P3, K3. Repeat from * to last 5 stitches, P3, K2.

Row 3: P2. *K3, P3. Repeat from * to last 5 stitches, K3, P2.

Row 4: Repeat row 2.

Row 5: K2. *YO, SL1, K2tog, PSSO, YO, K3. Repeat from * to last 5 stitches, YO, SL1, K2tog, PSSO, YO, K2.

Row 6: Repeat row 3.

Row 7: Repeat row 2.

Row 8: Repeat row 3.

Row 9: K2tog. *YO, K3, YO, SL1, K2tog, PSSO. Repeat from * to last 5 stitches, YO, K3, YO, SL1, K1, PSSO.

Next rows: Repeat rows 2-9 until piece is square. Bind off.

Photo for reference only: http://goo.gl/J5CrNk

DEWDROP PATTERN WASHCLOTH   November 24

Materials

Cotton worsted weight yarn

Knitting needles size 5.5mm

Directions

Row 1: Cast 37 stitches onto the needle.

Next rows: Work rows 2-9 of dewdrop pattern until piece is square. Bind off.

Photo for reference only: http://goo.gl/EAZyDr

Knitting a Diamond Rib Pattern November 25

Materials

Worsted weight yarn
Knitting needles for the project you are working on

Directions

Row 1: Cast 20 stitches onto the needle.
Row 2: With right side facing, P2. *K2tog, (K1, YO) twice, K1, SL1, K1, PSSO, P2. Repeat from * to end of row.
Row 3 and every odd row: I2. *P7, K2. Repeat from * to end of row.
Row 4: P2. *K2tog, YO, K3, YO, SL1, K1, PSSO, P2. Repeat from * to end of row.
Row 6: P2. *K1, YO, SL1, K1 PSSO, K1, K2tog, YO, K1, P2. Repeat from * to end of row.
Row 8: P2. *K2, YO, SL1, K2tog, PSSO, YO, K2, P2. Repeat from * to end of row.
Row 9: Repeat row 3.
Next rows: Repeat rows 2-9 until piece is square. Bind off.

Photo for reference only: http://goo.gl/a5KHku

Diamond Rib Leg Warmers November 26

Materials

1 skein Red Heart Super Saver worsted weight yarn

4 double pointed knitting needles size 5mm and 6mm

Directions

Round 1: Cast 66 stitches onto the smaller needle.
Next rounds: Work K1, P1 ribbing pattern all the way around. Repeat until piece measures 3".
Next rounds: Work rows 2-9 of diamond rib pattern until piece measures 15".
Next rounds: Work ribbing pattern until piece measures 18". Bind off.

Photo for reference only: http://goo.gl/f46qvD

Knitting an Alternating Feather Openwork Pattern November 27

Materials

Worsted weight yarn
Knitting needles for the pattern you are working on

Directions

Row 1: Cast 13 stitches onto the needle.
Row 2: With right side facing, K1. *K2tog, YO, K1, YO, SL1, K1, PSSO, K1. Repeat from * to end of row.

Row 3: Purl all the way across.

Rows 4-13: Repeat rows 2-3.

Row 14: K1. *YO, SL1, K1, PSSO, K1, K2tog, YO, K1. Repeat from * to end of row.

Row 15: Purl all the way across.

Next rows: Repeat rows 2-15 until piece is square. Bind off.

Photo for reference only: http://goo.gl/xrK8cl

*A*LTERNATING FEATHER OPENWORK SCARF   November 28

Materials

1 skein Red Heart Super Saver worsted weight yarn   Knitting needles size 6mm

Directions

Row 1: Cast 67 stitches onto the needle.

Next rows: Work rows 2-15 of alternating feather openwork pattern until piece reaches desired length. Bind off.

Finishing

Add a fringe to each end of the scarf.

Photo for reference only: http://goo.gl/V99e5O

*K*NITTING A FANCY OPENWORK PATTERN   November 29

Materials

Worsted weight yarn
Knitting needles for the project you are working on

Directions

Row 1: Cast 16 stitches onto the needle.

Row 2: With right side facing, K2. *YO, K4. Repeat from * to last 2 stitches, YO, K2.

Row 3: P2tog. **K1, P1) into the YO of previous row, (P2tog) twice. Repeat from * to last 5 stitches, (K1, P1) into the YO, P2tog.

Row 4: K4. *YO, K4. Repeat from * to end of row.

Row 5: P2, P2tog. *(K1, P1) in YO of previous row, (P2tog) twice. Repeat from * to last 5 stitches, (K1, P1) into the YO, P2tog, P2.

Next rows: Repeat rows 2-5 until piece is square. Bind off.

Photo for reference only: http://goo.gl/GWBFI6

FANCY OPENWORK PATTERN WASHCLOTH

Materials

Cotton worsted weight yarn

Knitting needles size 5.5mm

Directions

Row 1: Cast 36 stitches onto the needle.

Next rows: Work rows 2-5 of fancy openwork pattern until piece is square. Bind off.

Photo for reference only: http://goo.gl/OzJWzK

*T*HE PROS AND CONS OF USING KNITTING MACHINES

We can't write a knitting e-book without talking about knitting machines. A lot of people have been asking about whether or not they should be using knitting machines. Unfortunately, that is not something we can give you a definitive answer about. Ultimately, it depends on the knitter. Some knitters swear by using knitting machines, while others wouldn't touch one if you bought it for them and paid for all of their knitting supplies for the rest of their lives. What we can do is give you a rundown of the pros and cons of using knitting machines.

Knitting Machine Pros

Even though there are many knitters who prefer not to use knitting machines, those who do use them can't say enough good things about this knitting tool. The pros of using knitting machines include:

Speed – One of the things that users like best about knitting machines is how quickly they can create their projects.

Volume – Because they can knit faster with a machine, knitters can make many more items in shorter periods of time.

Intricacy – When using a knitting machine, you will be able to create some pretty intricate designs much easier than you can with regular knitting needles.

Less Hand Stress – A lot of knitters complain about pain in their hands. This is not an issue when you are using a knitting machine. You can do a lot of knitting without experiencing any pain at all.

Preset Patterns – Many knitters like the fact that knitting machines come with pre-set patterns. All they have to do is push a button, and the knitting begins.

Knitting Machine Cons

While there are a lot of advantages to using a knitting machine, there are also things that many knitters complain about. Some of the negative aspects of using a knitting machine include:

Patterns don't always Work – Often, patterns you choose will not translate well to knitting with a machine. Often, knitters must use a combination of machine knitting, hand knitting, and even crochet on certain projects.

Size – If you are considering getting a knitting machine, make sure that you have plenty of space for it. These machines are large and bulky, and they take up a lot of space.

Concentration – Unlike regular knitting, which many people can do without even looking at what they are doing, using a knitting machine requires intense concentration. You won't be able to just set your work down and pick it up again where you left off.

Practice – Before you really get the hang of using a knitting machine, you will have to do a lot of practice pieces. Many people get fed up at this point, sell their machines, and go back to regular knitting.

No Flexibility – You have to learn all of the machine settings, because you can't just switch from one type of stitch to another. You need to fiddle with the settings, which can take a while until you are used to it.

Cost – Knitting machines are expensive. Make sure that this is something you really want to get into before spending a lot of money.

December

Santa Claus is coming to town this month. Are you ready for the holidays? This month, we are offering up loads of great knitting patterns for holiday decorations, stocking stuffers, gifts, and more. You won't be at a loss for gifts for anyone on your list with this assortment of patterns. We even have a pattern for cute holiday stockings to fill with awesome knitted gifts.

OOT CUFFS

Materials

Worsted weight yarn
3 double pointed knitting needles size 5mm

Directions

Row 1: Cast 56 stitches onto the needle.
Row 2: K1, P1 all the way around.
Row 3: Repeat row 2 until piece measures 1".
Next rows: Knit all the way across. Continue working in garter stitch until piece measures 5".
Next rows: K1, P1 all the way around. Repeat rib stitch until piece measures 6". Bind off.

Photo for reference only: http://goo.gl/QLgIhx

CABLE PATTERN BOOT CUFFS

Materials

Worsted weight yarn

3 double pointed knitting needles size 5mm

Directions

Row 1: Cast 56 stitches onto the needle.
Row 2: K1, P1 all the way around.
Row 3: Repeat row 2 until piece measures 1".
Next rows: Work in cable stitch pattern until piece measures 5".
Next rows: Repeat row 2 until piece measures 6". Bind off.

Photo for reference only: http://goo.gl/f6nZqD

SEED STITCH FINGERLESS GLOVES

Materials

1 skein Red Heart Super Saver worsted weight yarn

Knitting needles size 5mm
Yarn needle

Directions

Make 2
Row 1: Cast 40 stitches onto the needle.
Row 2: Knit all the way across.
Next rows: Work in seed stitch pattern until piece measures 2".
Next rows: Work in stockinette stitch until piece measures 7".

Next rows: Work in seed stitch pattern until piece measures 9".

Finishing

Stitch along one side of each glove, placing the thumb hole in the stockinette stitch section.

Photo for reference only: http://goo.gl/sJnKy7

HOLIDAY SCARF   December 4

Materials

1 skein each red and green Red Heart worsted weight yarn

Knitting needles size 6mm

Directions

Row 1: Cast 65 stitches onto the needle with red yarn.
Rows 2-5: Knit all the way across.
Row 6: Knit all the way across.
Row 7: K4, P to last 4 stitches, K4.
Next rows: Repeat rows 6 and 7 until piece measures 6".
Next rows: Switch to green yarn and repeat rows 6 and 7 for 6". Continue working in this pattern until scarf reaches desired length. Bind off loosely.

Finishing

Pull yarn on each end of scarf to gather it in. Make a green and red tassel for each end of the scarf.

Photo for reference only: http://goo.gl/EmxAPK

CANDY CANE SCARF   December 5

Materials

1 skein each red and white Red Heart Super Saver yarn

Knitting needles size 6.5mm

Directions

Row 1: Cast 70 stitches onto the needle with white yarn.
Row 2: Knit all the way across.
Row 3: Repeat row 2.
Rows 4-5: Switch to red yarn, knit all the way across.
Next rows: Repeat rows 2-5 until piece reaches desired length. Bind off.

Finishing

Add a fringe to each end of the scarf.

Photo for reference only: http://bit.ly/22cr2TX

Warm Cowl

Materials

2 balls super chunky yarn
Knitting needles size 10mm

Yarn needle

Directions

Row 1: Cast 70 stitches onto the needle, loosely.
Row 2: Knit all the way across.
Next rows: Repeat row 2. Bind off loosely.

Finishing

Fold piece in half and stitch seam.

Photo for reference only: http://goo.gl/tXUMXJ

Easy Arm Warmers

Make 2

Materials

1 skein Red Heart Super Saver worsted weight yarn

Knitting needles size 4mm
Yarn needle

Directions

Row 1: Cast 36 stitches onto the needle.
Row 2: Knit all the way across.
Row 3: Purl all the way across.
Next rows: Continue working in stockinette stitch until piece measures 12". Bind off.

Finishing

Fold each piece in half, right sides facing, and stitch up the side. Turn right side out.

Photo for reference only: http://bit.ly/1Rfl6lb

Leg Warmers

Materials

1 skein Red Heart Super Saver worsted weight yarn

Knitting needles sizes 5 mm and 6mm
Yarn needle

Directions

Make 2
Row 1: Cast 66 stitches onto smaller needles.

Row 2: *K2, P2. Repeat from * to end of row.
Next rows: Repeat row 2 until piece measures 3". Switch to larger needles.
Next rows: Work in stockinette stitch until piece measures 15". Switch to smaller needles.
Next rows: Repeat row 2 until piece measures 18". Bind off.

Finishing

Fold each piece lengthwise, wrong sides together. Stitch the side seam and turn inside out.

Photo for reference only: http://goo.gl/ICm4jx

CABLE STITCH LEG WARMERS   December 9

Materials

1 skein Red Heart Super Saver worsted weight yarn

Knitting needles sizes 5 mm and 6mm
Yarn needle

Directions

Make 2
Row 1: Cast 66 stitches onto smaller needles.
Row 2: *K2, P2. Repeat from * to end of row.
Next rows: Repeat row 2 until piece measures 3". Switch to larger needles.
Next rows: Follow cable stitch pattern until piece measures 15". Switch to smaller needles.
Next rows: Repeat row 2 until piece measures 18".

Finishing

Fold each piece lengthwise, wrong sides together. Stitch the side seam and turn inside out.

Photo for reference only: http://bit.ly/21oVyYy

STRIPED LEG WARMERS   December 10

Materials

2 skeins Red Heart Super Saver worsted weight yarn, different colors

Knitting needles sizes 5 mm and 6mm
Yarn needle

Directions

Make 2
Row 1: Cast 66 stitches onto smaller needles with color A.
Row 2: *K2, P2. Repeat from * to end of row.
Next rows: Repeat row 2 until piece measures 3". Switch to larger needles.
Next row: Knit all the way across with color B.
Next row: Purl all the way cross.
Next row: Knit all the way across.
Next 3 rows: Repeat last 3 rows with color A.

Next rows: Continue working in a striping pattern until piece measures 15". Switch to smaller needles.

Next rows: Repeat row 2 until piece measures 18". Bind off.

Finishing

Fold each piece lengthwise, wrong sides together. Stitch the side seam and turn inside out.

Photo for reference only: https://goo.gl/WJU167

Holiday Table Runner December 11

Materials

1 skein each red and green Red Heart Super Saver worsted weight yarn

Knitting needles size 6mm

Directions

Row 1: With green yarn, cast 70 stitches onto the needle.

Rows 2-5: Knit all the way across.

Row 6: K4, switch to red yarn, K to last 4 stitches, K4 with green yarn.

Next rows: Repeat row 6 until piece measures 36'48".

Next 4 rows: Switch to red yarn and knit all the way across. Bind off.

Finishing

Add a red and green fringe to either end of the table runner.

Photo for reference only: http://goo.gl/8QeCSr

Baby Santa Hat December 12

Materials

Red and white worsted weight yarn
3 double pointed knitting needles size 6.5mm

Yarn needle

Directions

Round 1: Cast 40 stitches onto the needle with white yarn.

Rounds 2-7: *K2, P2. Repeat from * to end of row. Switch to red yarn.

Next rounds: Work in stockinette stitch until piece measures 5".

Next round: *K2, K2tog. Repeat from * to end of round.

Next round: Purl all the way around.

Next round: *K1, K2tog. Repeat from * to end of round.

Next round: Purl all the way around.

Next round: K2tog all the way around. Pull yarn through remaining stitches and pull tight to close the opening.

Finishing

Add a white pompom to the top of the hat.

Photo for reference only: http://goo.gl/wBIPfk

Holiday Ear Warmers   December 13

Materials

1 skein Red Heart Super Saver worsted weight yarn, variegated red, white, and green

Knitting needles size 6mm
Yarn needle

Directions

Row 1: Cast 16 stitches onto the needle.
Row 2: *K2, P2. Repeat from * to end of row.
Next rows: Repeat row 2 until piece is long enough to wrap around your head and ears. Bind off.

Finishing

Fold piece in half and stitch the seam.

Photo for reference only: https://goo.gl/nlrcP7

Holiday Gift Bags   December 14

Materials

Sparkly yarn, red and green
Knitting needles size 5mm

Yarn needle
Crochet hook

Directions

Row 1: Cast 40 stitches onto the needle in either color yarn.
Row 2: Knit all the way across.
Rows 3-6: Repeat row 2.
Next rows: Work in stockinette stitch until piece measures 19".
Next 5 rows: Knit all the way across. Bind off.

Finishing

Fold piece in half so the knitted rows line up with each other. Stitch along the side seams. Crochet a chain measuring 10", and weave it through the top section of the gift bag.

Photo for reference only: https://goo.gl/Y2z1hy

Cowl Head Scarf

Materials

Red Heart Super Saver worsted weight yarn

Knitting needles size 8mm
Yarn needle

Directions

Row 1: Cast 70 stitches onto the needle.
Row 2: *K2, P2. Repeat from * to end of row.
Next rows: Repeat row 2 until piece measures at least 48". Bind off.

Finishing

Fold piece in half, and stitch 12" from the beginning of the fold. Add a fringe to either end of the scarf sections.

Photo for reference only: http://goo.gl/wuH3OK

Holiday Placemats

Materials

Red and green worsted weight yarn

Knitting needles size 6mm or size to give a gauge of 5 stitches per inch

Directions

Row 1: Cast 80 stitches onto the needle with red yarn.
Rows 2-5: Knit all the way across.
Row 6: K4 with red yarn, switch to green yarn, K to last 4 stitches, K4 with red yarn.
Next rows: Repeat row 6 until piece measures 12".
Next rows: Repeat row 2 with red yarn for 4 rows. Bind off.

Photo for reference only: http://goo.gl/atuhP7

Holiday Coasters

Materials

Red and green worsted weight yarn
Knitting needles size 6mm or size to give a gauge of 5 stitches per inch

Directions

Row 1: Cast 20 stitches onto needle with red yarn.
Rows 2-3: Knit all the way across.
Row 4: K2, switch to green yarn, K to last 2 stitches, K2 with red yarn.
Next rows: Repeat row 4 until piece measures 3.75".

Next rows: Repeat row 2 with red yarn for 2 rows. Bind off.

Photo for reference only: https://goo.gl/4jSVXi

Basket Weave Stitch Leg Warmers December 18

Materials

1 skein Red Heart Super Saver worsted weight yarn
Knitting needles sizes 5 mm and 6mm
Yarn needle

Directions

Make 2
Row 1: Cast 66 stitches onto smaller needles with color A.
Row 2: *K2, P2. Repeat from * to end of row.
Next rows: Repeat row 2 until piece measures 3". Switch to larger needles.
Next rows: Work in basket weave stitch until piece measures 15". Switch to smaller needles.
Next rows: Repeat row 2 until piece measures 18". Bind off.

Finishing

Fold pieces in half lengthwise with right sides facing, and stitch along side seam. Turn right side out.

Photo for reference only: https://goo.gl/l8xA50

Bell Ornament December 19

Materials

Scraps of worsted weight yarn
Knitting needles size 6mm
Crochet hook

Jingle bell
Yarn needle

Directions

Row 1: Cast 12 stitches onto the needle.
Rows 2-7: Knit all the way across.
Row 8: K2tog, K4, K2tog, K4.
Row 9: Purl all the way across.
Row 10: K2tog all the way across. Bring yarn through remaining stitches and pull tightly, leave a long tail.

Finishing

Attach tail yarn at top of bell to crochet hook, and crochet a chain measuring 3". Stitch last chain stitch into first chain stitch to create a loop. Stitch a jingle bell to the bottom section of the piece.

Photo for reference only: http://goo.gl/BqXHu2

CANDY CANE ORNAMENT

Materials

Scraps of red and white worsted weight yarn

Knitting needle size 6mm
Starch (equal parts white glue and water)

Directions

Row 1: Cast 8 stitches onto the needle with white yarn.

Next rows: Work I-cord stitch for 2 rows.

Next row: K4, place these stitches on holder. Pick up red yarn and K4. Place these stitches on another holder.

Next rows: Pick up white and work I-cord stitch until piece measures 8". Repeat with red side.

Next rows: Twist red and white pieces around each other. Pin in place if necessary. Knit ends together and bind off.

Finishing

Soak piece in starch, and allow to dry overnight.

Photo for reference only: http://goo.gl/aecRdH

CHRISTMAS TREE ORNAMENT

Materials

Scraps of green worsted weight yarn
Knitting needles size 5mm
Crochet hook

Colored beads or sequins
Needle and thread

Directions

Row 1: Cast 4 stitches onto the needle.

Rows 2-5: Work in stockinette stitch.

Row 6: Cast on 6 stitches, K4, cast on 6 stitches.

Next rows: Working in stockinette stitch, decrease 1 stitch at the beginning and end of each row until there are 6 stitches remaining, ending on knit row.

Next row: Cast on 4 stitches, P4, cast on 4 stitches.

Next rows: Working in stockinette stitch, decrease 1 stitch at the beginning and end of each row until there are 4 stitches remaining, ending on knit row.

Next row: Cast on 4 stitches, P4, cast on 4 stitches.

Next rows: Working in stockinette stitch, decrease 1 stitch at the beginning and end of each row until there are 2 stitches remaining, ending on knit row.

Next row: P2tog. Place crochet hook in remaining stitch, and crochet a chain measuring 3". Connect last chain stitch to first chain stitch to form a loop.

Finishing

Sew beads or sequins to the tree to make the ornaments.

Photo for reference only: http://goo.gl/e8Niqa

STUFFED SNOWMAN ORNAMENT December 22

Materials

Scraps of white and red worsted weight yarn
3 double pointed knitting needles size 4.25mm
Knitting needles size 4.25mm

Buttons (for eyes, nose, and buttons on body)
Needle and thread
Fiberfill stuffing

Directions

Round 1: Cast 24 stitches onto the needles.
Rounds 2-25: Knit all the way around.
Round 26: *K1, K2tog. Repeat from * to end of round.
Round 27: *K1, K2tog. Repeat from * to last stitch, K1.
Round 28: *K1, K in front and back of next stitch. Repeat from * to last stitch, k1.
Round 29: *K1, K in front and back of next stitch. Repeat from * to end of round.
Rounds 30-40: Knit all the way around.
Round 41: *K1, K2tog. Repeat from * to end of round.
Rounds 42-44: K2tog all the way around. Stuff snowman body and head with fiberfill stuffing.
Round 45: K2tog, bind off. Attach crochet hook, and crochet a chain measuring 3". Connect to first stitch of chain to create a loop.

Finishing

With red yarn and straight needles, cast on 5 stitches. Knit all rows until piece measures about 12-14". Tie around snowman's neck. Use buttons and scraps of red thread to create face and buttons on front of body.

Photo for reference only: http://goo.gl/gYsKd6

HOLIDAY GIFT TAGS December 23

Materials

Scraps of red and white worsted weight yarn
Knitting needles size 6mm

Glitter glue
1/8" satin ribbon

Directions

Row 1: Cast 10 stitches onto the needle.
Row 2: Knit all the way across.

Row 3: Purl all the way across.
Next rows: Work in stockinette stitch until piece measures 3", ending on a purl row.
Next row: K2tog, K6, K2tog.
Next row: P2tog, P4, K2tog.
Next row: K2tog, P2, K2tog. Bind off.

Finishing

Run a piece of ribbon through the point section of the tag and tie to create a loop for hanging. Use the glitter glue to write the recipients' names on the tags.

Photo for reference only: http://goo.gl/NQPwWB

HOLIDAY HAND WARMERS   December 24

Materials

Red and white worsted weight yarn   Yarn needle
Knitting needles size 6mm

Directions

Make 2
Row 1: Cast 33 stitches onto the needle.
Row 2: *K1, P1. Repeat from * to end of row.
Row 3: *P1, K1. Repeat from * to end of row.
Next rows: Repeat rows 2 and 3 until piece measures 2".
Next row: Increase 1 stitch, K to last stitch, increase 1 stitch.
Next row: Purl all the way across.
Next row: Knit all the way across.
Next rows: Contine working in stockinette stitch until piece measures 6-7". Bind off.

Finishing

Fold piece in half lengthwise. Stitch side seam, leaving space for a thumbhole.

Photo for reference only: http://goo.gl/I8m8Ve

GINGERBREAD MAN ORNAMENT   December 25

Materials

Brown worsted weight yarn   Yarn needle
Scraps of white worsted weight yarn   Crochet hook
Knitting needles size 6mm

Directions

Row 1: Cast 3 stitches onto the needle with brown yarn. Leave a long tail for chain loop.
Row 2: Knit.

Row 3: K1, M1, K1, M1, K1.

Rows 4-5: Knit.

Row 6: K1, M1, K3, M1, K1.

Rows 7-9: Knit.

Row 10: SSK, K3, K2tog.

Row 11: Knit.

Row 12: SSK, K1, K2tog.

Rows 13-14 (neck): Knit.

Next rows (arms and body): Cast on 8 stitches at the beginning of each of the next 2 rows.

Next 3 rows: Knit.

Next row: Bind off 5 stitches at the beginning of each of the next 2 rows.

Next 3 rows: Knit.

Next row: K1, M1, K7, M1, K1.

Next 2 rows: Knit.

Next row: SSK, K7, K2tog.

Next row (legs): K4. Put remaining stitches onto a stitch holder.

Next 2 rows: Knit.

Next row: K2tog, K1, M1, K1.

Next row: Knit.

Next row: K2tog, K1, M1, K1.

Next row: Knit and bind off.

Next row (other leg): Put stitches on holder back onto needle. Attach yarn where you did the bind off, and knit to the end of the row.

Next 2 rows: Knit.

Next row: SSK, K7, K2tog.

Next row (legs): K4. Put remaining stitches onto a stitch holder.

Next 2 rows: Knit.

Next row: K2tog, K1, M1, K1.

Next row: Knit.

Next row: K2tog, K1, M1, K1.

Next row: Knit and bind off.

Finishing: Use the scraps of white yarn to stitch on details. Use tail at top of head to crochet a chain loop for hanging.

Photo for reference only: http://goo.gl/Qm9IWW

*F*AST AND EASY POTHOLDER   December 26

Materials

1 skein worsted weight yarn
Knitting needles size 6.5mm
Crochet hook

Directions

Row 1: Using 2 strands of yarn, cast 20 stitches onto the needle.

Row 2: Right side facing, K10, seed stitch 10.

Row 3: Seed stitch 10, K10.

Next rows: Repeat rows 2 and 3 until piece measures 3.5", ending on wrong side.

Next row: Reverse pattern. 10 seed stitch, K10.

Next row: K10, 10 seed stitch.

Next rows: Repeat last 2 rows until piece measures 7". Bind off and use tail to crochet a chain loop for hanging.

Photo for reference only: https://goo.gl/Xfxxn8

KNITTED HANDBAG December 27

Materials

Worsted weight yarn
Knitting needles size 5mm

1 piece Velcro
Needle and thread

Directions

Row 1: Cast 30 stitches onto the needle.

Row 2: Knit all the way across.

Next rows: Repeat row 2 until piece measures 12".

Next row (flap): P2, K to last 2 stitches, P2.

Next row: knit all the way across.

Next rows: Repeat the last 2 rows until flap section measures 1.5", ending on a row 1.

Next row: K2, K2tog, K to last 4 stitches, K2tog, K2.

Next row: P2, K2tog, K to last 4 stitches, K2tog, P2.

Next row: Repeat last 2 rows until there are 8 stitches remaining, ending on a row 2.

Next row: P2, K2tog twice, P2.

Next row: K1, K2tog twice, K1. Bind off.

Finishing

Mark piece at the beginning of the flap, and fold up to that point. Stitch the side seams. Turn right side out, and stitch Velcro in place on the front and under the flap.

Photo for reference only: https://goo.gl/OzQOp1

HAIR BOW December 28

Materials

Scraps of worsted weight yarn
Knitting needles size 5mm
Hair clip

Glue gun and glue

Directions

Row 1: Cast 12 stitches onto the needle.
Row 2: Knit all the way across.
Next rows: Repeat row 2 until piece is about 1-1.5" wide. Bind off.

Finishing

Wrap a piece of yarn around the center of the knitted piece several times to create the "knot" in the center of the bow. Glue a hair clip to the back of the bow.

Photo for reference only: http://goo.gl/xsQoou

Kitty Cape   December 29

Materials

Red Heart Super Saver worsted weight yarn

Knitting needles size 9mm
Crochet hook

Directions

Row 1: Cast 22 stitches onto the needle.
Rows 2-4: *K1, P1. Repeat from * to end of row.
Row 5: Knit all the way across, increasing one stitch for each stitch on the needles.
Next rows: Knit all the way across each row until piece measures about 8-10", depending on the size of your cat. Bind off loosely.

Finishing

Crochet 2 chains about 8" in length, and attach to the each end of the neck ribbing section of kitty cape.

Photo for reference only: https://goo.gl/8hVdPu

Easy Infinity Scarf   December 30

Materials

2 skeins chunky or bulky yarn

Circular knitting needle size 15mm

Directions

Round 1: Cast 90 stitches onto the needle.
Round 2: *K2, P1. Repeat from * to end of round.
Round 3: Repeat round 2.
Round 4: Purl all the way around.
Next rounds: Repeat rounds 2-4 7 times.
Next round: *K2, P1. Repeat from * to end of round. Bind off using the same K2, P1 pattern.

Photo for reference only: http://goo.gl/29gl8u

PRACTICE SQUARE AFGHAN

Materials

Worsted weight yarn
Practice stitch squares

Yarn needle

Directions

Stitch all of your practice squares to form a lap blanket or afghan. If you need to make it bigger, or you need to fill in some spaces, simply make more practice squares and stitch them on.

Finishing

Add a fringe all the way around the blanket, or use a crochet hook to create a pretty edge all the way around.

CONCLUSION

We hope you have enjoyed trying out the patterns in this e-book, and that the articles will be great reference tools for you to use on future knitting projects. Knitting is a fun and relaxing hobby that anyone can do, and it isn't just limited to women. In fact, men and children should be encouraged to take up this hobby. Not only is it a great way to relax, it is a good way to be able to create their own clothing, decorative items, and so much more.

If you have done all of the patterns in this e-book, don't fret. We have another 45 patterns for you in a bonus mini-book. That will get you knitting into the next year, and of course, you will likely end up repeating a lot of patterns in this book and in the mini-book. Once people see the items that you make, you can be pretty sure that they are going to ask you to repeat the patterns for them. Have fun, and happy knitting.

Bonus 45 Knitting Pattern

1 NTRODUCTION

Oh no! You ran out of knitting patterns to work on, but you can't get enough of this fun hobby. Don't worry, we have 45 more fun patterns for you to work on. You will find all kinds of easy patterns that you can make up in a few hours (or less), as well as more fancy knitting stitches to add to your skills.

KNITTING AN ELONGATED STITCH PATTERN

Materials

Worsted weight yarn
Knitting needles for the project you are working on

Directions

Row 1: Cast 16 stitches onto the needle.
Rows 2-3: Knit all the way across.
Row 4: With right side facing, K6. *(YO) twice, K1, (YO) 3 times, K1, (YO) 4 times, K1, (YO) 3 times, K1, (YO) twice, K6.
Row 5: Knit all the way across, dropping the YO's from the needles.
Rows 6-7: Knit all the way across.
Row 8: K1. Repeat row 3 from * to last stitch, K1.
Row 9: Repeat row 5.
Next rows: Repeat rows 2-9 until piece is square. Bind off.

Photo for reference only: http://goo.gl/B6ihQX

ELONGATED STITCH SCARF

Materials

1 skein Red Heart Super Saver worsted weight yarn
Knitting needles size 6mm

Directions

Row 1: Cast 66 stitches onto the needle.
Next rows: Work rows 2-9 of elongated stitch pattern until piece reaches desired length. Bind off.

Photo for reference only: http://goo.gl/UhHSK3

SEED STITCH DISHCLOTH

Materials

Cotton worsted weight yarn   Knitting needles size 5.5mm

Directions

Row 1: Cast 35 stitches onto the needle.
Row 2: Knit all the way across.
Row 3: Knit all the way across.
Row 4: K2, follow seed stitch to last 2 stitches, K2.
Next rows: Repeat row 4 until piece is square.
Last 2 rows: Knit all the way across. Bind off.

Photo for reference only: http://goo.gl/S9zA9b

SLIP STITCH DISHCLOTH

Materials

Cotton worsted weight yarn

Knitting needles size 5mm

Directions

Row 1: Cast 37 stitches onto the needle
Row 2: *K1, yarn in front, SL1, yarn in back. Repeat from * to last stitch, K1.
Row 3: K1, P to last stitch, K1.
Row 4: K1. *K1, yarn in front, SL1, yarn in back. Repeat from * to last stitch, K1.
Row 5: K1, P to last stitch, K1.
Next rows: Repeat rows 2-5 until piece is square. Bind off.

Photo for reference only: http://goo.gl/Xoyp8S

KNITTING A VERTICAL DROP STITCH PATTERN

Materials

Worsted weight yarn

Knitting needles for the project you are working on

Directions

Row 1: Cast 20 stitches onto the needle.
Row 2: With right side facing, K1. *P2, K1, YO, P2, K2. Repeat from * to last 3 stitches, P2, K1.
Rows 3, 5, and 7: P1. *K2, P2, K2, P3. Repeat from * to last 3 stitches, K2, P1.
Rows 4 and 6: K1. *P2, K3, P2, K2. Repeat from * to last 3 stitches, P2, K1.
Row 8: K1. *P2, K1, drop next stitch off needle and unravel 6 rows beneath stitch, K1, P2, K1, YO, K1. Repeat from * to last 3 stitches, P2, K1.
Rows 9, 11, and 13: P1. *K2, P3, K2, P2. Repeat from * to last 3 stitches, K2, P1.
Rows 10 and 12: K1. *P2, K2, P2, K3. Repeat from * to last 3 stitches, P2, K1.
Row 14: K1. *P2, K1, YO, K1, P2, K1, drop next stitch and unravel 6 rows beneath stitch, K1. Repeat from * to last 3 stitches, P2, K1.
Next rows: Repeat rows 2-14 until piece is square. Bind off.

Photo for reference only: http://goo.gl/N8WKU9

VERTICAL DROP STITCH SCARF

Materials

1 skein Red Heart Super Saver worsted weight yarn
Knitting needles size 6.5mm

Directions

Row 1: Cast 68 stitches onto the needle.

Next rows: Work rows 2-14 of vertical drop stitch pattern until piece reaches desired length. Cast off.

Finishing

Add a fringe to each end of the scarf.

Photo for reference only: http://goo.gl/5sGsFT

Cute Cowl

Materials

2 skeins super chunky yarn
Knitting needles size 9mm

Yarn needle

Directions

Row 1: Cast 25 stitches onto the needle.

Row 2: SL1 knitwise, K to end of row.

Next rows: Repeat row 2 until piece measures 18". Bind off.

Finishing

Fold piece in half, but place ends so only half of each end touches the other, leaving an assymetrical edge.

Photo for reference only: http://goo.gl/Q0SGgW

Simple Beanie

Materials

1 skein Red Heart Super Saver worsted
weight yarn

Knitting needles size 5mm
Yarn needle

Directions

Row 1: Cast 84 stitches onto the needle.

Row 2: With right side facing, *K1, P1. Repeat from * to end of row.

Row 3: *P1, K1. Repeat from * to end of row.

Next rows: Repeat rows 2-3 until piece measures 7", ending on a wrong side row.

Row 1 of decrease: K1. *P3tog, (K1, P1) 9 times, K3tog, (P1, K1) 9 times. Repeat from * to last stitch, P1.

Row 2 and all alternate rows: *P1, K1. Repeat from * to end of row.

Row 3: K1. *P3tog, (K1, P1) 8 times, K3tog, (P1, K1) 8 times. Repeat from * to end of row.

Row 5: K1. *P3tog, (K1, P1) 7 times, K3tog, (P1, K1) 7 times. Repeat from * to end of row.

Row 7: K1. *P3tog, (K1, P1) 6 times, K3tog, (P1, K1) 6 times. Repeat from * to end of row.

Row 9: K1. *P3tog, (K1, P1) 5 times, K3tog, (P1, K1) 5 times. Repeat from * to end of row.

Row 11: K1. *P3tog, (K1, P1) 4 times, K3tog, (P1 K1) 4 times. Repeat from * to end of row.

Row 13: K1. *P3tog, (K1, P1) 3 times, K3tog, (P1 K1) 3 times. Repeat from * to end of row.

Row 15: K1. *P3tog, (K1, P1) twice, K3tog (P1 K1) twice. Repeat from * to end of row.

Row 17: K1. *P3tog, K1, P1, K3tog, P1, K1. Repeat from * to end of row. Draw yarn through remaining stitches and pull tight to close opening. Bind off.

Finishing

Stitch back seam.

Photo for reference only: http://goo.gl/HKGOIb

Garter/Stockinette Stitch Scarf

Materials

1 skein Red Heart Super Saver worsted weight yarn

Knitting needles size 4mm

Directions

Row 1: Cast 75 stitches onto the needle.

Row 2: Knit all the way across.

Rows 3-11: Repeat row 2.

Row 12: Purl all the way across.

Rows 13, 15, 17, 19, and 21: Knit all the way across.

Rows 14, 16, 18, and 20: Purl all the way across.

Rows 22-31: Repeat rows 2-11.

Rows 32-41: Repeat rows 12-21.

Next rows: Repeat both patterns until piece reaches desired length. Bind off.

Photo for reference only: http://goo.gl/wH2BDm

Knitting an Interlaced Stitch Pattern

Materials

Worsted weight yarn
Knitting needles for the project you are working on

Directions

Row 1: Cast 16 stitches onto the needle.

Rows 2-5: Knit all the way across.

Row 6: K1. *Insert needle into next stitch and wrap yarn around needle 4 times, knit stitch withdrawing all wraps with the needle. Repeat from * to last stitch, K1.

Row 7: *SL8 stitches with yarn in back, dropping extra loops (creating 8 long stitches on right needle), insert left needle into first 4 of these 8 stitches, pass them over the second 4 stitches, return all stitches to left needle, knit the 8 stitches in the following order: 2nd and 4th stitches first, then the original 4 stitches. Repeat from * to end of row.

Rows 8-11: Knit all the way across.

Row 12: Repeat row 6.

Row 13: SL4 stitches, dropping extra wraps, cross 2 over 2 as with row 7, K these 4 stitches. *SL8, cross, K as with row 7. Repeat from * to end of row.

Next rows: Repeat rows 2-13 until piece is square. Bind off.

Photo for reference only: http://goo.gl/Xk7mz6

INTERLACED STITCH INFINITY SCARF

Materials

1 skein Red Heart Super Saver worsted weight yarn

Knitting needles size 6mm
Yarn needle

Directions

Row 1: Cast 64 stitches onto the needle.

Next rows: Work rows 2-13 of interlaced stitch pattern until piece measures 36". Bind off.

Finishing

Fold piece in half and stitch ends together.

Photo for reference only: http://goo.gl/6QvaJf

KNITTING A SHADOW CHEVRON STITCH

Materials

Worsted weight yarn
Knitting needles for the project you are working on

Directions

Row 1: Cast 17 stitches onto the needle.
Row 2: K1. *P1, K1. Repeat from * to end of row.
Row 3: P1. *K7, P1. Repeat from * to end of row.
Row 4: K2. *P5, K3. Repeat from * to last 7 stitches, P5, K2.
Row 5: K2. *K5, P3. Repeat from * to last 7 stitches, K5, P2.
Row 6: K3. *P3, K5. Repeat from * to last 6 stitches, P3, K3.
Row 7: P3. *K3, P5. Repeat from * to last 6 stitches, K3, P3.
Row 8: K4. *P1, K7. Repeat from * to last 5 stitches, P1, K4.
Row 9: P4. *K1, P7. Repeat from * to last 5 stitches, K1, P4.
Row 10: P1. *K7, P1. Repeat from * to end of row.
Row 11: K1. *P7, K1. Repeat from * to end of row.
Row 12: P2. *K5, P3. Repeat from * to last 7 stitches, K5, P2.
Row 13: K2. *P5, K3. Repeat from * to last 7 stitches, P5, K2.
Row 14: P3. *K3, P5. Repeat from * to last 6 stitches, P3, K3.
Row 15: K3. *P3, K5. Repeat from * to last 6 stitches, P3, K3.

Row 16: P4. *K1, P7. Repeat from * to last 5 stitches, K1, P4.
Row 17: K4. *P1, K7. Repeat from * to last 5 stitches, P1 4.
Next rows: Repeat rows 2-17 until piece is square. Bind off.

Photo for reference only: http://goo.gl/4TteV6

Shadow Chevron Stitch Placemat

Materials

Worsted weight yarn   Knitting needles size 6mm

Directions

Row 1: Cast 65 stitches onto the needle.
Next rows: Work rows 2-17 of shadow chevron stitch pattern until piece measures 10". Bind off.

Photo for reference only: http://goo.gl/B5bl1q

Knitting a Branch Lace Pattern

Materials

Worsted weight yarn   Knitting needles for the project you are
                                             working on

Directions

Row 1: Cast 21 stitches onto the needle.
Row 2: *P1, K2, K2tog, YO, K1, YO, SSK, K2. Repeat from * to last stitch, P1.
Row 3: K1. *P1, P2tog through back loop, YO, P3, YO, P2tog. Repeat from * to last stitch, K1.
Row 4: *P1, K2tog, YO, K5, YO, SSK. Repeat from * to last stitch, P1.
Row 5: K1. *P9, K1. Repeat from * to end of row.
Next rows: Repeat rows 2-5 until piece is square. Bind off.

Photo for reference only: http://goo.gl/jwBoKw

Branch Lace Pattern Scarf

Materials

1 skein Red Heart Super Saver worsted weight yarn
Knitting needles size 6.5mm

Directions

Row 1: Cast 71 stitches onto the needle.
Next rows: Work rows 2-4 of branch lace pattern until piece reaches desired length. Bind off.

Finishing

Add a fringe to each end of the scarf.

Photo for reference only: http://goo.gl/lPNbMM

KNITTING A GABLES LACE PATTERN

Materials

Worsted weight yarn
Knitting needles for the project you are working on

Directions

Row 1: Cast 21 stitches onto the needle.
Row 2: With right side facing, K1. *YO, SSK, K2tog, YO, K1. Repeat from * to end of row.
Row 3 and all odd rows: Purl all the way across.
Row 4: Repeat row 2.
Row 6: K1. *YO, SSK, K5, K2tog, YO, K1. Repeat from * to end of row.
Row 8: K1. *K4, YO, SSK, K1, K2tog, YO, K2. Repeat from * to end of row.
Row 10: K1. *K2, YO, SSK, K1, K2tog, YO, K3. Repeat from * to end of row.
Row 12: K1. *K3, YO, CDD, YO, K4. Repeat from * to end of row.
Row 13: Purl all the way across.
Next rows: Repeat rows 2-13 until piece is square. Bind off.

Photo for reference only: http://goo.gl/FPmj87

GABLES LACE WASHCLOTH

Materials

Cotton worsted weight yarn   Knitting needles size 6mm

Directions

Row 1: Cast 41 stitches onto the needle.
Next rows: Work rows 2-13 of gables lace pattern until piece is square. Bind off.

Photo for reference only: http://goo.gl/rbY0mY

STRIPED BEANIE

Materials

Worsted weight yarn, 5 colors   Yarn needle
Knitting needles size 5.5mm

Directions

Row 1: Cast 74 stitches onto the needle.

Rows 2-7: *K1, P1. Repeat from * to end of row.

Row 8: Knit all the way across.

Row 9: Purl all the way across.

Next rows: Repeat rows 8-9, alternating yarn colors, until piece measures 7", ending with a purl row.

Next row: K2tog all the way across.

Next row: Purl all the way across.

Next row: K2tog all the way across. Pull thread tightly through remaining stitches to close opening.

Finishing

Stitch back seam.

Photo for reference only: http://goo.gl/9ywuZV

SIMPLE BABY BLANKET

Materials

DK baby weight yarn   Circular knitting needles size 4mm

Directions

Row 1: Work back and forth instead of in rounds. Cast 186 stitches onto the needle.

Row 2: *K2, P2. Repeat from * to last 2 stitches, K2.

Row 3: *P2, K2. Repeat from * to last 2 stitches, P2.

Row 4: Repeat row 3.

Row 5: Repeat row 2.

Row 6: K2, P2, K9. *P1, K2, P1, K8. Repeat from * to last 5 stitches, K1, P2, K2.

Row 7: P2, K2, P to last 4 stitches, K2, P2.

Row 8: P2, K11. *P1, K2, P1, K8. Repeat from * to last 5 stitches, K3, P2.

Row 9: K2, Purl to last 2 stitches, K2.

Next rows: Repeat rows 2-9 until piece is square. Bind off.

Photo for reference only: http://goo.gl/6MNldV

SIMPLE BABY BLANKET 2

Materials

DK weight baby yarn   Circular knitting needles size 4mm

Directions

Row 1: Work back and forth instead of in rounds. Cast 187 stitches onto the needle.

Row 2: *K1, P1. Repeat from * to last stitch, K1.

Rows 3-5: Repeat row 2.

Row 6: (K1, P1) twice, K5. *P1, K5. Repeat from * to last 4 stitches, (P1, K1) twice.

Row 7: K1, P1, K1, P to last 3 stitches, K1, P1, K1.

Rows 8-11: Repeat rows 5-6 twice.

Row 12: Repeat row 2.

Row 13: Repeat row 7.

Next rows: Repeat rows 2-13 until is square. Bind off.

Photo for reference only: http://goo.gl/C9KYD9

Checkered Afghan Square

Materials

Worsted weight yarn, 2 colors   Knitting needles size 5.5mm

Directions

Row 1: Cast 18 stitches onto the needle with main color.

Row 2: Knit all the way across.

Row 3: Knit 3 with MC, K3 with Color B, K3 MC, K3 color B, K3 MC.

Row 4: P3 with color B, K3 main color, P3 color B, K3 main color, P3 Color B.

Next rows: Repeat rows 2-4 until piece is square. Bind off.

Photo for reference only: http://goo.gl/KpYzcD

Checkered Afghan

Materials

2 skeins Red Heart Super Saver worsted weight yarn, 2 colors
Knitting needles size 5.5mm

Directions

Row 1: Cast 18 stitches onto the needle with main color.

Next rows: Work rows 2-4 of checkered afghan square pattern until piece is square. Bind off.

Finishing

Make as many squares as you need to complete an afghan. You may make the squares larger or smaller if you wish. Add a fringe all the way around.

Photo for reference only: http://goo.gl/QZCMMM

Links and Posts Afghan Square

Materials

Worsted weight yarn
Knitting needles size 6mm

Directions

Special stitches: Right Cross (2X2RC) – SL next 2 stitches onto cable needle and hold in back, K2 from left needle K2 from cable needle. Left Cross (2X2LC) – SL next 2 stitches onto cable needle and hold in front, K2 from left needle, K2 from cable needle.

Row 1: Cast 36 stitches onto the needle.

Rows 2-7: Knit all the way across.

Row 8: With right side facing, K3, P1, K1, (M1, K13) twice, M1, K1, P1, K3.

Row 9: K4, P to last 4 stitches, K4.

Row 10: K3, P1, (K4, YO, SSK, K1, K2tog, YO) 3 times, K4, P1, K3.

Row 11: K4, P to last 4 stitches, K4.

Row 12: K3, P1, 2X2LC, K1, YO, SL2-K1-P2sso, YO, K1, 2X2LC, K1, YO, SL2-K1-P2sso, YO, K1, 2X2RC, K1, YO, SL-2-K1-P2sso, YO, K2, 2X2RC, P1, K3.

Row 13: K4, P to last 4 stitches, K4.

Next rows: Repeat rows 2-13 until piece is square. Bind off.

Photo for reference only: http://goo.gl/7cqFwy

LINKS AND POSTS AFGHAN

Materials

3 skeins Red Heart Super Saver worsted weight yarn
Knitting needles size 6mm
Yarn needle

Directions

Row 1: Cast 36 stitches onto the needle.

Next rows: Work rows 2-13 of links and posts pattern until piece is square. Bind off.

Finishing

Make as many squares as you need for the size afghan you want. Stitch squares together.

Photo for reference only: http://goo.gl/QO2e3e

PLAID STITCH PATTERN

Materials

3 colors of worsted weight yarn   Knitting needles size 6mm

Directions

Row 1: Cast 21 stitches onto the needle with Color A.

Rows 2-4: Knit all the way across.

Row 5: K3, P3 with main color, P1 Color B, P3 Color A, P1 Color C, P3 Color A, P1 Color B, P3 Color C, K3 Color A.

Row 6: Repeat row 5, reversing K's for P's and vice versa.

Row 7: K3 Color A, P3 with Color B, K1 Color C, K3 Color B, K1 Color C, K3 Color B, K1 Color C, K3 Color B, K3 Color A.

Row 8: K3 Color A, P to last 3 stitches Color C, K3 Color A.

Row 9: K3 Color A, K3 Color A, K1 Color C, K3 Color A, K1 Color C, K3 Color A, K1 Color C, K3 Color A, K3 Color A.

Rows 10-11: Repeat row 9.

Next rows: Repeat rows 2-11 until piece is almost square.

Last 3 rows: Knit all the way across with Color A.

Photo for reference only: http://goo.gl/WaO1jI

PLAID STITCH SCARF

Materials

3 colors worsted weight yarn

Knitting needles size 6mm

Directions

Row 1: Cast 72 stitches onto the needle.

Rows 2-4: Knit all the way across.

Next rows: Work rows 2-11 of plaid stitch pattern until piece reaches desired length.

Last 3 rows: Knit all the way across.

Photo for reference only: http://goo.gl/SWFpga

KNITTING A TEXTURED HEART PATTERN

Materials

Worsted weight yarn
Knitting needles for the project you are working on

Directions

Row 1: Cast 15 stitches onto the needle.

Row 2: *(P1, K1). Repeat from * to last stitch, P1.

Row 3: Purl all the way across.

Row 4: *P1, K6, P1, K6. Repeat from * to end of row.

Row 5: P1. *P5, K3, P6. Repeat from * to end of row.

Row 6: *P1, K4, P2, K1, P2, K4. Repeat from * to last stitch, P1.

Row 7: P1. *P3, K2, P3, K2, P4. Repeat from * to end of row.

Row 8: *P1, K2, P2, K5, P2, K2. Repeat from * to last stitch, P1.

Row 9: P1. *P1, K2, P3, K1, P3, K2, P2. Repeat from * to end of row.

Row 10: *P1, K1, P2, K2, P3, K2, P2, K1. Repeat from * to last stitch, P1.

Row 11: P1. *P2, K4, P1, K4, P3. Repeat from * to end of row.

Row 12: *P1 K3, P2, K3, P2, K3. Repeat from * to last stitch, P1.

Row 13: Purl all the way across.

Next rows: Repeat rows 2-13 until piece is square. Bind off.

Photo for reference only: http://goo.gl/ZcPDgm

*T*EXTURED HEART COWL

Materials

2-3 skeins super chunky yarn   Circular knitting needles size 9mm

Directions

Row 1: Cast 57 stitches onto the needle.
Next rows: Work rows 2-13 of textured heart pattern until piece measures 18". Bind off.

Photo for reference only: http://goo.gl/bpd5ZM

*K*NITTING AN OPENWORK LADDER PATTERN

Materials

Worsted weight yarn   Knitting needles for the project you are working on

Directions

Row 1: Cast 16 stitches onto the needle.
Row 2: K6. *P2, K1, P1 K6. Repeat from * to end of row.
Row 3: P6. *K2tog through back loop, (YO) twice, K2tog, P6. Repeat from * to end of row.
Row 4: K6. *P2, K1, P1, K6. Repeat from * to end of row.
Next rows: Repeat rows 2-4 until piece is square. Bind off.

Photo for reference only: http://goo.gl/JreKXo

*O*PENWORK LADDER BABY BLANKET

Materials

1 skein Red Heart Super Saver worsted weight yarn   Circular knitting needle size 6mm
Crochet hook

Directions

Row 1: Work back and forth instead of in rounds. Cast 96 stitches onto the needle.
Next rows: Work rows 2-4 of openwork ladder pattern until piece reaches desired size. Bind off.

Finishing

Crochet a shell border around the edge as follows: *3 double crochet in 1 stitch, skip a stitch. Repeat from * all the way around.

Photo for reference only: http://goo.gl/9uy6Kx

KNITTING A BEADED RIB STITCH

Materials

Worsted weight yarn
Knitting needles for the project you are working on

Directions

Row 1: Cast 17 stitches onto the needle.
Row 2: With right side facing, P2. *K1, P1, K1, P2. Repeat from * to end of row.
Row 3: K2. *P3, K2. Repeat from * to end of rw.
Next rows: Repeat rows 2-3 until piece is square. Bind off.

Photo for reference only: http://goo.gl/vOMHGK

BEADED RIB STITCH SCARF

Materials

1 skein Red Heart Super Saver worsted weight yarn
Knitting needles size 6.5mm

Directions

Row 1: Cast 67 stitches onto the needle.
Next rows: Work rows 2-3 of beaded rib stitch pattern until piece reaches desired length. Bind off.

Finishing

Add a fringe to each end of the scarf.

Photo for reference only: http://goo.gl/Sc090c

KNITTING A BIBA TRELLIS STITCH

Materials

Worsted weight yarn
Knitting needles for the project you are working on

Directions

Row 1: Cast 19 stitches onto the needle.
Row 2: With right side facing, purl all the way across.
Row 3: Knit all the way across.
Row 4: Repeat row 2.
Row 5: P1. *P7, SL3, P4. Repeat from * to last 4 stitches, P4.
Row 6: k4. *K4, SL3, K7. Repeat from * to last stitch, K1.
Rows 7-8: Repeat rows 5-6.

Row 9: Repeat row 5.
Rows 10-12: Repeat rows 2-4.
Row 13: P1, SL3. *P11, SL3. Repeat from * to last stitch, P1.
Row 14: K1, SL3. *K11, SL3. Repeat from * to last stitch, K1.
Rows 15-16: Repeat rows 13-14.
Next rows: Repeat rows 2-16 until piece is square. Bind off.

Photo for reference only: http://goo.gl/T07xXZ

Biba Trellis Stitch Placemat

Materials

Worsted weight yarn   Knitting needles size 6.5mm

Directions

Row 1: Cast 75 stitches onto the needle.
Next rows: work rows 2-16 of biba trellis stitch pattern until piece measures 9-10". Bind off.

Photo for reference only: http://goo.gl/LUQ59U

Boot Cuffs

Materials

Worsted weight yarn
3 double pointed knitting needles size 5.5mm

Directions

Make 2
Round 1: Cast 52 stitches onto the needle.
Rounds 2-11: *K2, P2. Repeat from * to end of round.
Round 12-25: Knit all the way across.
Rounds 26-35: Repeat round 2. Bind off.

Photo for reference only: http://goo.gl/rvSrQt

Corset Laced Leg Warmers

Materials

1 skein Red Heart Super Saver worsted
weight yarn

4 double pointed knitting needles sizes
5mm and 6mm
¼" ribbon

Directions

Make 2

Round 1: Cast 64 stitches onto the smaller needle.
Round 2: *K2, P2. Repeat from * to end of round.
Next rounds: Repeat round 2 until piece measures 3"
Next rounds: Switch to larger needle and knit all the way around.
Next rounds: Repeat last round until piece measures 15".
Next Rounds: Repeat round 2 until piece measures 18". Bind off.

Finishing

Lace ribbon in a criss-cross manner up the front of each leg warmer.

Photo for reference only: https://goo.gl/dHkR8x

Corset Laced Arm Warmers

Materials

Worsted weight yarn
3 double pointed knitting needles size 5mm
¼" ribbon

Directions

Make 2
Round 1: Cast 34 stitches evenly onto the needles.
Round 2: *K1, P1. Repeat from * to end of round.
Next rounds: Repeat round 2 until piece measures 1.5".
Next rounds: Work in stockinette stitch until piece measures 8.5".
Next rounds: Repeat round 2 until piece measures 10". Bind off.

Finishing

Lace ribbon in a criss-cross manner up the front of each arm warmer.

Photo for reference only: https://goo.gl/DjqJXM

Knitting a Country Grove Stitch

Materials

Worsted weight yarn
Knitting needles for the project you are working on

Directions

Row 1: Cast 15 stitches onto the needle.
Row 2 and all even rows: With right side facing, K all the way across.
Row 3: Repeat row 2.
Rows 5 and 7: P3. *K3, P3. Repeat from * to end of row.
Rows 9 and 11: K all the way across.

Rows 13 and 15: K3. *P3, K3. Repeat from * to end of row.
Row 16: Repeat row 2.
Next rows: Repeat rows 2-16 until piece is square. Bind off.

Photo for reference only: http://goo.gl/sNt3AR

COUNTRY GROVE STITCH LEG WARMERS

Materials

1 skein Red Heart Super Saver worsted weight yarn
4 double pointed knitting needles sizes 5mm and 6mm

Directions

Make 2
Round 1: Cast 63 stitches onto the smaller needle.
Round 2: K1. *P2, K2. Repeat from * to last stitch, K1.
Next rounds: Repeat round 2 until piece measures 3".
Next rounds: Work rows 2-16 of country grove stitch pattern until piece measures 15".
Next rounds: Repeat round 2 until piece measures 18". Bind off.

Photo for reference only: http://goo.gl/Aosks9

KNITTING A CROSSROADS PATTERN

Materials

Worsted weight yarn
Knitting needles for the project you are working on

Directions

Row 1: Cast 14 stitches onto the needle.
Row 2: K4, P6. *K6, P6. Repeat from * to last 4 stitches, K4.
Row 3: P4, K6. *P6, K6. Repeat from * to last 4 stitches, P4.
Row 4: K2. *P2, K6, P2, K2. Repeat from * to end of row.
Row 5: P2. *K2, P6, K2, P2. Repeat from * to end of row.
Rows 6-11: Repeat last 2 rows, 3 times.
Rows 12-13: Repeat rows 2-3.
Row 14: Knit all the way across.
Row 15: Purl all the way across.
Next rows: Repeat rows 2-15 until piece is square. Bind off.

Photo for reference only: http://goo.gl/X1AiY1

CROSSROADS PATTERN SCARF

Materials

1 skein Red Heart Super Saver worsted weight yarn
Knitting needles size 6mm

Directions

Row 1: Cast 74 stitches onto the needle.
Next rows: Work rows 2-15 of crossroads pattern until piece reaches desired length. Bind off.

Finishing

Add a fringe to each end of the scarf.

Photo for reference only: http://goo.gl/hv0clw

STRIPED WASHCLOTH

Materials

Cotton worsted weight yarn, 3 colors   Knitting needles size 5mm

Directions

Row 1: Cast 45 stitches onto the needle with Color A.
Row 2: Knit all the way across.
Row 3: K3, P to last 3 stitches, K3.
Rows 4-7: Repeat rows 2 and 3.
Next rows: Continue repeating rows 2-3, switching colors after every 3 rows.
Last row: Knit all the way across.

Photo for reference only: http://goo.gl/TwjFxk

FUN COWL

Materials

Super chunky yarn   Circular knitting needle size 10mm

Directions

Round 1: Cast 54 stitches onto the needle.
Round 2: *K1, P1. Repeat from * to end of round.
Round 3: *P1, K1. Repeat from * to end of round.
Round 4: Repeat round 2.
Round 5: Repeat round 3.
Rounds 6-9: Knit all the way across.
Next rounds: Repeat rounds 2-9 twice.

Next rounds: Repeat rounds 2-5 twice. Bind off.

Photo for reference only: http://goo.gl/JJl3oe

CHEMO CAP

Materials

1 ball chunky yarn

4 double pointed knitting needles size 5.5mm

Directions

Round 1: Cast 60 stitches onto the needle.
Round 2: *K8, K2tog. Repeat from * to end of round.
Round 3 and all odd rounds: Knit all the way across.
Round 4: *K7, K2tog. Repeat from * to end of round.
Round 6: *K6, K2tog. Repeat from * to end of round.
Round 8: *K5, K2tog. Repeat from * to end of round.
Round 10: *K4, K2tog. Repeat from * to end of round.
Round 12: *K3, K2tog. Repeat from * to end of round.
Round 14: *K2, K2tog. Repeat from * to end of round.
Round 16: *K1, K2tog. Repeat from * to end of round.
Round 18: K2tog all the way around. Bind off.

Photo for reference only: http://goo.gl/ds18EC

SAMPLE SQUARE BABY BLANKET

Materials

Knitting stitch practice squares
Worsted weight yarn for stitching

Yarn needle

Directions

Stitch all of the squares together. If you need more to make the blanket even, make them in any stitch pattern you like.

Finishing

Add a fringe all the way around blanket.

CONCLUSION

We hope that you have enjoyed these additional 45 simple knitting patterns. Once you get the hang of the specialty stitches, you can use them for all kinds of other patterns, and even create your own customized knitting patterns.

Printed in the USA
CPSIA information can be obtained
at www.ICGtesting.com
LVHW022256300723
753893LV00041B/1253